FRIENDS & LOVERS

SAM & GERI LAING

FRIENDS & Lovers

Marriage
As God Designed It

DPI
DISCIPLESHIP
PUBLICATIONS
INTERNATIONAL

One Merrill Street
Woburn, MA 01801
1-800-727-8273
Fax: (617) 937-3889

Friends and Lovers
©1996 by Discipleship Publications International
One Merrill Street, Woburn, MA 01801

Printed in the United States of America

Cover design & illustration: Chris Costello
Interior layout: Chris Costello and Laura Root
Back cover photo: Charles McKelvey

ISBN 1-884553-95-8

For our children:
Elizabeth, David, Jonathan and Alexandra.
You are our joy and our crown.

"I was married and lived
      happily ever afterwards."

-WINSTON CHURCHILL

Contents

Acknowledgments

We express our deepest appreciation to our many friends who have patiently assisted us during the six months in which this book was written. To our staff members who have carried a heavier load, you have our undying gratitude. To our personal assistant, Tracy MacLachlan, for your initiative, positive attitude and service beyond the call of duty we are deeply grateful. Our daughter Elizabeth made invaluable contributions throughout the writing and editing process, and we give her our love and thanks. To all of our friends at Discipleship Publications International, whose work is far more than a job, but is a labor of love and a ministry for Jesus Christ, we love and respect you always.

Introduction

I met the two greatest friends of my life as winter turned to spring in my nineteenth year. They are my best friends now and will remain so forever. And since it was the first friend who led me to the second, to the young woman I am about to describe to you, I am everlastingly in his debt.

Without my knowing it, he arranged for our meeting to take place at a church retreat. It had been my custom to go to such affairs with mixed motives—partially to search for spiritual answers and partially to meet attractive young women. On the drive out to the retreat site that Friday afternoon, my conscience was afire with guilt over my double-mindedness. Only a few weeks previous, I had made my decision to commit my life wholeheartedly to God, and this less than pure motive was a discouraging reappearance of my supposedly forsaken old self. I asked my companion driving the car to pull over so we could talk. I opened my heart, shed tears of sorrow and resolved that this retreat would be different—God and his purposes would be first in my mind. No more looking for girls!

I changed clothes—out of my spiffy suede cowboy boots and stylish shirt, into old sneakers and a bland, marginally shabby, synthetic golf shirt. I meant business.

I arrived at the retreat with a soul cleansed of guilt, a mind free of distraction and a heart ready for spiritual inspiration. A small crowd began to gather.

It was then that I saw her for the first time. I stopped dead in my tracks. I could not tear my eyes away. She was beautiful. Radiant. Sparkling. Innocent. Warm. Full of life, gladness and joy. I could see it, sense it and feel it all the way across the crowded room. When she smiled her eyes glittered, her face shone, and the room seemed to brighten. Her laughter was like music. I had never seen anyone more lovely in soul and in form; I have not since, nor will I ever again.

My conscience suddenly flared with sobering accusation: What of my promise? Had I already forgotten it? Did I come here to serve my own purposes or God's? My spirits plunged, but I knew I must honor my earlier decision. I gathered my emotions, turned away and carried on as if I had seen nothing. I was later briefly introduced to her, but cordially made my exit and gave my attention to the events that lay ahead.

The retreat was magnificent. I found myself growing in faith and drawing closer to the group of students who shared my new-found commitment. As events drew to a close on Saturday, I allowed myself a few moments with her. We talked about what we had learned and what we wanted to do with our lives. I shared with her the story of my recent decision— of being raised in a lifeless religion and of finding my faith after a long battle with selfishness and skepticism. She listened carefully and said she was now undergoing a similar search and longed to arrive at the same place I had.

I returned to school that evening and resisted the impulse to pick up the phone and arrange to see her. (She was visiting from out of town and had stayed to attend services the next morning.) I decided to wait. I saw her that Sunday morning as she prepared to leave: an unremarkable conversation, a brief good-bye, and she was on her way home.

Weeks later, I called her. I was not sure if she would remember who I was. She did. I wrote her. She wrote back. She told me she had decided to withdraw from her college and move to be with the church where I was because of its strong spiritual base. She wanted to find God.

The next fall, she arrived and became a part of the struggling young group of college students in that small, but visionary, church. Three and one half years later we were married. Almost twenty-five years after that, with four children and a lifetime of memories, tears and laughter, we are still together, and will be until we die. She is the greatest gift I have in this world; she is my friend and my lover for life.

To whom do I owe this gift? Who was the other friend, the one who led us to each other? He was the friend I had met just a few weeks before I met her—he was the Father in heaven who found me, and whom I found, after a long and painful search. Although I resisted, he drew me by the integrity, wonder, righteousness and love that I saw in his matchless Son. Out of the depths of my selfishness and skepticism, I made the decision to love him long after he had graciously chosen to love me. And, after I gave to him the place of supremacy in my heart, he gave me the woman who is the greatest blessing of my life. He is my greatest friend of all.

We write this book because God has given us our lives and our marriage. We do not deserve what we have. We do not believe we have a perfect marriage or that we know all the answers. But we know who has given us everything good that we enjoy, and in these pages we offer something back of what we have so freely received.

<hr />

> "Therefore everyone who hears these words of mine and puts them into practice is like a wise man who built his house on the rock" (Matthew 7:24).

This is a book to teach you what a great marriage is and to help you build one. It is our conviction that Planet Earth came with an owner's manual—the Bible. Therefore, everything taught in our book will, in one way or another, come out of the pages of the Scriptures. We will present in the following chapters the wonderful concept of marriage: We as couples are to be friends and lovers. Each of us who marries is committed for life to this member of the opposite sex who is our best friend and who shares with us the intimacies of sexual love. But before we go any further, let us set forth the principles upon which a great marriage is built.

Commitment to God

The foundation of a great marriage is our personal and joint relationship with God. This relationship comes about through decisions we make individually to become disciples of Jesus Christ (Luke 9:23). So much of what we will say in this book is based on this assumption. Many of you are in other situations. Perhaps neither of you has ever become a disciple of Jesus, or perhaps you have fallen from your original commitment to him. Others of you are in a marriage where only one partner is a disciple. Certain principles taught in the Bible (and in this book) will produce better marriages even for those who are not personally committed to Christ, but the ultimate impact will be limited until both of you dedicate your individual lives and your marriage to God. God intends us to live our lives and base our marriages upon the rock of his Word—that is the only sure way to a joyful life and a great marriage. That is why the best thing you can do for your relationship with each other is to make a decision to seek God. Without such a conviction you will find many of the principles taught in this book impossible or difficult to apply.

Commitment to One Another

The Bible teaches that we are to be faithful to our spouses until death. When we marry, God, in some mysterious and spiritual way that we do not understand, knits us together into one person. He intends the bond to be permanent. Jesus once was asked if God allowed divorce. He replied that God made allowance only for marital unfaithfulness:

> "Haven't you read," he replied, "that at the beginning the Creator 'made them male and female,' and said, 'For this reason a man will leave his father and mother and be united to his wife, and the two will become one flesh'? So they are no longer two, but one. Therefore what God has joined together, let man not separate" (Matthew 19:4-6. See also vv. 7-10.)

There is an all-too-prevalent attitude that we should simply give up on a marriage when it is difficult or when we just don't feel like trying anymore. Even if we have the most serious of problems, we still do not have reason to quit! *Even in the case of adultery, divorce is permitted, but not necessarily required or encouraged.* I have seen many marriages salvaged gloriously from the wreckage of adultery.

Therefore I would urge you to ban all talk of divorce. Even in moments of frustration and anger, never utter the word. Always assume and believe you are going to stay together and work things out. Marriage is for life!

Commitment to Making It on Our Own

> For this reason a man will leave his father and mother and
> be united to his wife, and they will become one flesh
> (Genesis 2:24).

We should always honor our fathers and mothers, but there comes a time when we must set out on our own and build a life for ourselves. We must establish our emotional, physical, financial and social independence from our parents. If we live in close proximity to either set of in-laws, we must be sure to establish our own marriage, household and family life. Too many of us have never grown up. We go running back to Mom and Dad for a financial or emotional bailout when things get tough. If this is your attitude and practice, you will never have a great marriage.

Your parents should be included in your lives and in your children's lives as well. But what is best for your folks is your building your own life so that when the time comes, you can help support them as they once supported you.

Commitment to Recommitment

Most of us on our wedding day were excited, happy and deeply in love. In all likelihood, we gave our hearts completely to each other. But hearts can be damaged, dulled and distracted. True love is sustained by continual recommitment. Though we once made the decision to love, we must remake it many times. When you see your spouse at his or her weakest, you must give your heart again. When you are tempted to offer your affections to another person, you must reject such thoughts and give your heart once more to your only true love. When life's worst blows have broken you, give your heart as always to your true friend and lover. When your children cry for attention, you must first love your husband or wife. When your mate has hurt you and has failed to meet your needs, you still must give him or her your heart. And you must give it again and again and again....

It amazes me how hard we work at less important things. We go to school to learn to make a living, drive an automobile, acquire new hobbies, or prepare a tax return—but we do not take the time and effort to learn how to build our most important human relationship. My challenge to you is to put in the time, effort, tears, prayer, work and sweat it will take to construct a great marriage. It will pay dividends beyond your wildest dreams!

✦

We close these introductory thoughts with three convictions we have that we hope will become yours as well:

- Any two people can change.
- Any marriage can be fixed.
- Any marriage can become great.

We don't know where your marriage is today, but wherever it is, we are confident that what we will share with you in the following pages can make a difference. This book is for those who are not married but want help in getting ready. It is for those who feel their marriage is good but want to find ways to make it better. It is for those who started with sizzle, but now are wondering where they lost it. It is for those who got off to a poor start and have never found a way to turn it around. It is for those who have hurt each other so much they wonder if their relationship is beyond repair.

Whatever has happened, you cannot go back and change the past. But you can learn and press forward and build on a new foundation. The time to begin is now.

Sam and Geri Laing
Cary, North Carolina
May 1996

PART

1

· Relationship ·

CHAPTER 1

Friends & Lovers

His mouth is sweetness itself;
he is altogether lovely.
This is my lover, this my friend,
O daughters of Jerusalem.

SONG OF SONGS 5:16

B est friends. Exciting lovers. Rarely has the heart and soul of marriage been summed up any better. Friendship and romantic love are the two essential ingredients of a great marriage, the qualities that will make it grow ever richer, deeper and more fulfilling. Although this should be the norm, few of us grew up seeing such marriages, and perhaps even fewer of us believed that we could experience such a relationship ourselves. Many have seen marriage as a drain rather than a fountainhead, a battleground instead of a refuge, and a pit stop rather than a permanent home.

Put aside your preconceptions, your problems and your past. Above all, get rid of your low expectations. A marriage relationship between two people who are friends and lovers is not just for the gifted, the beautiful or the few. It is intended for everyone, including you. The only thing stopping you is your doubt. It is time to lay faithlessness aside and get on with the business of building your marriage.

Let us begin with the foundation. What role should marriage play in our lives?

Our Lifetime Companions

> The LORD God said, "It is not good for the man to be alone.
> I will make a helper suitable for him" (Genesis 2:18).

Human beings are social creatures. The Creator himself said that it is not good for us to be alone—he made us to crave the companionship of others. Loneliness haunts us. We reach out to understand and to be understood. Without someone we deeply know and who deeply knows us, we are left incomplete, with a gaping void in our hearts that gnaws at us and slowly consumes us, stealing from us the very joy of life. God in his mercy has therefore provided the marriage relationship as a way to quench this fundamental thirst for secure, consistent, lifetime companionship.

Our spouses should be our best friends on earth. They should know our minds, hearts, souls and feelings more than anyone else does. They, above all others, are the people whom we love to be with, talk to or just sit in silence with, and with whom we share life's day-to-day experiences, heartbreaks and joys.

This is the only relationship in life that we must remain in until one of us is taken by death. We should honor our parents, but we are not intended to live with them always—we are to leave them and build a life with our spouses (Genesis 2:24). Likewise, our children one day will leave us. Friends are indispensable and we need as many as we can acquire, but circumstances inevitably move them in and out of our daily lives. Only our marriage partners stay beside us for life. We are to be committed to each other—to be together and to stay together in a secure, abiding friendship that will last until death.

The Foundation of Accomplishment

If we are married, the strength of that marriage is the basis of a powerful, effective life. Our ability to accomplish is magnified amazingly when we have our spouses at our sides supporting us and working with us. Happy are those who recognize that marriage is teamwork, that we are better together than we are apart! If you look carefully, you will see that most of us marry someone quite different from us in temperament and personality. This is by God's design and is a part of the

genius and mystery of marriage—although we all have weaknesses, our spouses' strengths can often make up for them.
Working together as one, we each become the person we never
would have become on our own.

> Two are better than one,
>   because they have a good return for their work:
> If one falls down,
>   his friend can help him up.
> But pity the man who falls
>   and has no one to help him up!
> Also, if two lie down together, they will keep warm.
>   But how can one keep warm alone?
> Though one may be overpowered,
>   two can defend themselves.
> A cord of three strands is not quickly broken
> (Ecclesiastes 4:9-12).

If we seek to build a life of accomplishment upon the
foundation of a weak, faltering marriage, we build upon sink-
ing sand. Neglecting our marriages undercuts everything else
we hope to attain. Stories abound of men and women in public life who have lost the confidence and respect of their followers because of a failed private life. Some may have even
achieved a measure of success while living in a difficult marriage, but could have done so much more with the confidence,
joy and respect a great marriage would have given them.

Many of us, however, have our priorities reversed. We feel
that in order to succeed we must pour ourselves into our ca-
reers, even at the expense of our marriages. But this is actually one of the most self-destructive choices we could make.
People who do this end up in bitterness, cynicism and sadness, knowing they have lost the love of their most important
friend and the love of their children as well. Success in other
endeavors is never enough to overcome the damage caused
by a failed marriage.

In addition, the Bible requires that those with ambitions of
leading people spiritually have strong marriages and families:

> Here is a trustworthy saying: If anyone sets his heart on
> being an overseer, he desires a noble task. Now the over-
> seer must be above reproach, the husband of but one wife,

> temperate, self-controlled, respectable, hospitable, able to
> teach, not given to drunkenness, not violent but gentle,
> not quarrelsome, not a lover of money. He must manage
> his own family well and see that his children obey him
> with proper respect. (If anyone does not know how to
> manage his own family, how can he take care of God's
> church?) (1 Timothy 3:1-5; see also verses 6-13).

Unfortunately, there are many who claim leadership of
God's people, but have failed at home. The Bible disqualifies
them as true leaders, because who they are at home is who
they really are. Those who pass the test of building excellent
families are the genuine leaders who have earned the right to
show others the way.

The Fulfillment of Our Sexuality

> For this reason a man will leave his father and mother and
> be united to his wife, and they will become one flesh
> (Genesis 2:24).

Sex is one of the most powerful forces in the world. It
inspires, frustrates, satisfies, mystifies and torments us. A quick
perusal of the music, art and literature of the ages shows its
pervasive influence on human life and history. By it we define
our coming of age, and by it many judge their own (and others') intrinsic worth. For large numbers of people, the search
for sexual fulfillment and satisfaction is the dominant pursuit
of life.

God created sex and sexuality. He made us male and female, and instructed that we become "one flesh." If you have
not yet figured out that those words are talking about sex in
marriage please read on! God did not make a mistake when
he invented sex—it was a part of the great design—a design
to perpetuate the human race, to give himself glory, and to
give us joy, happiness and fulfillment.

The marriage of a man and a woman who become lifetime friends and lovers is God's plan for our sexual contentment. It is a great plan, an ingenious plan, a plan that works
in real life; and it is high time many of you married couples
began to enjoy it! One of the great aims of the book is to

present the beautiful concept of sexual love in marriage and to inspire you to embrace it in your own relationship. It is so important that we will devote a major section (Chapters 5-7) to discussing it fully.

But not only is sex in marriage God's great plan; it is also the *only* plan. There is no other option. When we ignore and defy God's design, we experience untold ruin, misery and degradation. Perhaps nothing in all the world has caused more deeply felt pain, heartache and misery than the abuse of sexuality. The solution to our sexual frustrations and difficulties is not abandoning God's great concept of romance in marriage, but learning how to make it work for us!

A Place to Build a Family

> God blessed them and said to them, "Be fruitful and increase in number; fill the earth..." (Genesis 1:28).

God created marriage and family to be the setting in which children are conceived, born and raised. Family is to be the fundamental unit of all society. He intends young ones to be brought up in an environment that is secure, loving and spiritual. Children who are raised by parents who have a relationship of genuine love and respect and a happy sexual union are much more likely to someday grow up to be productive and happy themselves.

Society is now reaping a bitter harvest for failing to follow this course in years past. The increasing number of children born out of wedlock is an ominous portent of social chaos and terror to come. Many of today's young people have incredible emotional difficulties caused directly by the breakdown of their parents' relationship or the lack of a two-parent household. Because they have been unloved, hurt and abandoned, they do not understand the meaning of love or the value of human life, and they have not learned to respect the opposite sex. They have little trust in others, a limited capacity for forming permanent relationships, no identity and no conscience. And so the crime rate skyrockets and social breakdown accelerates at an alarming rate.

God intends for children to live at home under the protective, loving and guiding hand of their parents until they are old enough to go out and build a life on their own. The glory and joy of parenting is to raise children to become men and women of integrity and faith, children who honor their parents and care for them when they someday become too weak to care for themselves. God's plan is good, wise and powerful. We neglect it to our heartbreak, and we embrace it to our joy and fulfillment.

Friends and lovers! That is God's plan for marriage. We are to be best friends for life. We are to accomplish together what we could never do alone. We are to have an exciting, fulfilling sex life. We are to raise our children to be persons of character and integrity who will be a blessing to us in our old age. What God plans, he enables. What an awesome plan and what a great promise!

CHAPTER 2

Can We Talk?

The tongue has the
power of life and death....

PROVERBS 18:21

During my younger years, talking with me was, in the words of Winston Churchill, "...a riddle wrapped in a mystery inside an enigma." I had never learned to be comfortable sharing my deepest self with anyone. Many times I actually had no clue what my real feelings or thoughts were. (If we do not share them, thoughts and feelings become more buried and shrouded in mystery.) I would often become quiet and withdrawn. After I married, the question men so often hear—"What are you thinking?"—was frequently asked me by my wife. I would reply with a nervous "Oh, nothing important; I just have a few things on my mind." Now, *that* really helped to put Geri at ease! I finally improved to the point that I could say, "Honey, if it's something about you, I'll let you know." Well, that was better, but it still left Geri in the dark about what I was thinking, and in the end, it left her not knowing who I *really* was.

Life became increasingly more difficult for me because of my lack of communication. I grew discouraged and lonely as I withdrew further into myself. I felt trapped, a prisoner within my own private world. I bore my anxieties, fears, frustrations and questionings alone. I loved my wife profoundly, but there was a level of my self that I withheld from her. I am now sure that had I continued along this path, my marriage was headed for a terrible reckoning.

Finally I resolved to open up with Geri about my inner thoughts. I decided that since this woman loved me more than anyone on the face of God's earth, I would entrust her with the deepest, darkest part of my soul. I gathered up my courage, fortified my humility, and started talking.

Immediately I felt a great sense of relief. No longer did I have to carry the weight of my burdens alone. I now had at my disposal the matchless treasures of Geri's compassion, understanding and encouragement. Now she could use one of her greatest gifts—wisdom—in advising and helping me. We were a team at last! My honesty and humility helped Geri grow in confidence. I watched her blossom into a more mature and radiant woman as I finally allowed her to fulfill her role in our marriage. We drew amazingly close to each other. Geri truly became my best friend, something God had intended all along! Now, years later, I thank God for these changes and would not ever consider going back to the way we were. I believe my decision, to be and to remain open, is one of the greatest decisions I have ever made—one that has built the very foundation of my marriage!

How is the communication going in your marriage? Do you know and understand your spouse? Do you talk on a deep level, or do you limit your conversation to the superficial and mundane? Do you find yourself holding in what you would like to say? Are you frustrated? Are you afraid to talk about what is most important? Do you have difficulty putting your thoughts and feelings into words? Do you find that you are not even sure what your feelings and thoughts are? Is your idea of an open exchange limited to having an intense confrontation? When is the last time you had a heart-to-heart discussion with your spouse that was more than an angry scene? Are there things you have lied about to your spouse or deliberately withheld from him or her? How often do you just sit down and talk?

Let's face it: It is usually men who hold back in communication. For the most part, wives need to talk, want to talk, and try to talk. Most women would give anything if their husbands would stop and listen to them. But men so often do not hear. They do not talk. They sit in silence and superficiality. Let me call this masculine trait by several names it so richly deserves: *Arrogant. Hard-hearted. Ignorant. Foolish.* It is not a sign of strength to be this way. Talking with and listening to our wives is not the refuge of the emotional, effeminate or weak man—nor is it only a marginal need of the "manly" man. Men who think they don't need to talk are deceived. Men who think they have nothing to talk about are deceived. While we all possess different temperaments, *there is no man anywhere who does not need to open his heart to his wife, whether he feels the need or not.*

Having spoken forthrightly to the men, let me say that I find that most married people (men and women) lack pathetically in the area of sharing their real hearts with one another. Marriage can be no more satisfying or happy than the degree to which you open your heart and mind to your spouse. This is not just an option for those who want a certain type of marriage. It is a necessity for those who want to have a marriage—period. How can we be friends if we do not talk, and how can we be lovers if we are not friends? Many couples limp along with a superficial relationship for years. Then, one day the kids grow up and move away, leaving them alone with just each other, and alone with the chilling truth: *They are strangers living in the same house.*

Our message to you is that it does not have to be this way. You can change. Your spouse can change. You can build a relationship in which you communicate openly, consistently and deeply. It will take work. It will call for humility. It will demand self-denial and persistence. In a word, it will be challenging. But the rewards of a revived and renewed marriage are infinitely greater than the effort it will take to change.

But how do we do it? What are the attitudes, actions and habits that prevent real communication? What must we overcome to open the way to a true sharing of our hearts and lives? We will discuss in detail ten of the most common problems that can and will kill communication within our marriages.

Communication Killers

1. Failure to Listen

> My dear brothers, take note of this: Everyone should be
> quick to listen, slow to speak and slow to become angry
> (James 1:19).

Communication is a two-way street. It is far more than
merely saying what we want to say and getting our point
across—it means listening as well. If you are frequently preoccupied, often having to ask your spouse to repeat himself
or herself, then you are not listening. If you find yourself frequently saying things like: "What?" "Huh?" or "I don't remember that," you are probably not hard of hearing, just hard of
heart!

Some of us are great listeners—when the subject interests
us. We listen *selectively*. If the matters at hand are not important to us, we listen halfheartedly, tune out or change the subject. Our intensity of attention when we have personal interest highlights our apathy when we do not. This can frustrate
our spouses and tempt them to be resentful.

Not listening may seem to be only a small flaw, but it says
You are not really that important to me. Failure to listen is failure to show love and respect. We may excuse ourselves blithely
with, "Oh, I'm just preoccupied," but translated this means
our concern for ourselves is greater than our concern for the
other person.

Once again it is men who are the chief offenders (although
I have known some women who were notoriously poor listeners). I don't know why we excel in this communication flaw—
maybe men are always tired from work (but aren't women also?),
or perhaps male genetics are mysteriously predisposed towards
preoccupation and selfishness. But whatever the root, cause,
reason or excuse, men simply have a hard time paying attention to their wives—and this must change.

The way to change is...*just change!* Pledge that when your
spouse addresses you, you will stop what you are doing, change
your train of thought, look him or her in the eyes, and listen
lovingly and attentively to every word. (Husbands: In prepa-

ration for this change, buy some smelling salts to use in reviving your wife when she faints from shock!)

2. Defensive Listening

> He who answers before listening—
> that is his folly and his shame
> (Proverbs 18:13).

Defensive "listening" is done not to hear and consider the words of our spouses, but merely to give ourselves time to prepare a response. We never really give their opinions or feelings serious consideration. We even finish our spouses' phrases for them, as if they needed our quick minds to help them make it to the end of a sentence. Oh, we hate it when *they* do this—we can see the wheels turning behind their eyes even as we speak! Some of us are defensive even when no one is attacking. "What do you mean by *that*?" is our oft-repeated reply. Our tones of voice and reflexive outbursts belie a greater problem of pride. Instead of hearing what is said, we formulate our entire thinking process around protecting ourselves.

The root of this problem is pride. We are defensive because we assume we are right most of the time. "Don't confuse me with the facts—my mind is made up," is our motto. Have you ever stopped long enough to consider that your spouse could have a glimmer of insight? That he or she might even be right or have a better idea?

Defensiveness begets defensiveness. If you are defensive and stubborn, your spouse will either become a doormat (albeit a frustrated one!) or an opponent, always guarding himself or herself in preparation for the next verbal joust.

Geri and I once worked with a couple who were extremely defensive in their relationship, even on the smallest of issues. Both of them were emotional and opinionated. He would often express himself sarcastically, which hurt her feelings and led her to respond in kind. After a long period of observing and listening to them, we discovered that the husband actually had the more tender heart and was more willing to listen and change. It was the wife's arrogance that was the sticking point. She was defensive, haughty, and emotional with us even as we tried to counsel her. As Geri and I found ourselves getting provoked in our interactions with her, we realized the difficulties her husband faced. We challenged her. She reacted defensively (of course!). Her husband sat up a little straighter in his chair, with a new-found gleam of hope in his eye. We persisted. She reacted even worse, but eventually saw what we were saying. She became deeply ashamed of her pride, apologized to her husband, and resolved to change (as did he).

There are still occasional bumps in their relationship, but they are learning how to respectfully and patiently listen to one another. As a result, there is now peace between them that has never been there before.

3. Disrespect of Viewpoint

> A fool finds no pleasure in understanding
>   but delights in airing his own opinions
> (Proverbs 18:2).

Many of us have the attitude that we are always right, and that we know more than everyone else, especially more than our spouses. We snap off quick answers. The main exercise we get is by jumping to conclusions! We feel free to contradict and correct our mates—often in front of others. We say things like, "What she really means is…" or "Forgive my husband, he's so…." This is rude and embarrassing, and reveals an attitude of disrespect. If you find yourself repeatedly improving or altering what your husband or wife is saying, you have a real problem. Actually, you probably won't "find yourself" doing it at all—it is a longtime habit hidden within a smug superior disposition. In all likelihood, this communication flaw will need to be pointed out to you; you are not likely to see it on your own.

4. Cutting, Critical Remarks

> Do not let any unwholesome talk come out of your mouths,
> but only what is helpful for building others up according
> to their needs, that it may benefit those who listen
> (Ephesians 4:29).

The tongue that cuts, slashes and wounds is one of the most common, hurtful and lethal problems in marriage. It has many forms. It speaks with tainted tones of sarcasm and muffled mutterings of bitterness. It expresses itself with phony sincerity and with hurtful shouts, name-calling and cursing. It disguises its criticism with cruel humor, mockery and subtle jabs. And it shows itself in our body language of smirks, rolling eyes and shaking heads.

We justify ourselves in the name of honesty: "I always say exactly what I think." Or we subtly turn the tables: "Oh, I didn't realize you were so sensitive." In spite of how reasonable our excuses may sound to us, they ring hollow as we consider the inspired words of Scripture, "Love...is not rude" (1 Corinthians 13: 4-5).

I am appalled at the way I sometimes hear husbands and wives address each other. I have seen couples go at it to the point that I was embarrassed for them, but they went on with no shame. Many of us perhaps grew up around rude, cutting language and are not shocked by it. Perhaps some have spoken this way so long that they are desensitized to its brutal effect. Or it could be that they imitate the "slash and burn" standards of the TV sitcoms, where people rip into each other with sneering insults, put-downs, and sarcasm. Whatever the reason, there is *never* an excuse to speak in such a way as to retaliate, humiliate or denigrate. We must radically repent of such sinful speech. "Instead, speaking the truth in love, we will in all things grow up into him who is the Head, that is, Christ" (Ephesians 4:15).

5. Hinting

If rudeness is the weakness of some, obliqueness is the weakness of others. By this I mean an indirect, subtle hinting around what we really mean to say. We drop a hint here and there, then expect our mate to be a psychologist and mind reader rolled into one. And to top it off, if he or she does not figure it out, we get upset! We need to stop playing this selfish, immature game. It unfairly puts the burden upon our spouses to figure out what we already know and could express if we chose. It is a form of control and manipulation. If we are afraid to say what we mean, we need to muster the courage to speak our minds, remembering that our fears are usually fears of how *we*, not our mates, might be hurt.

6. *Clamming Up*

...Do not let the sun go down while you are still angry, and do not give the devil a foothold (Ephesians 4:26-27).

Some of us have a great way to avoid conflict—we clam up! We go for hours or days without really talking. When we are angry, hurt or afraid, we withdraw into a shell of self-protection. We simmer in anger, quiver in fear or wallow in self-pity. We solve nothing by this behavior. Shutting down can become a form of manipulation. By it we force our mates into a guessing game or into a guilt trip. We do this to put the burden upon them to figure out what is bothering us. What are our spouses to do? They can wear themselves out trying to get us to talk, blow up at us in frustration, or merrily go on their way, oblivious that we are upset.

If something is troubling you, you should let your spouse know. You need to pick the right time and place, but you must talk it out, or it will degenerate into bitterness and re-sentment. You must trust God's plan, which I would describe this way: *Get it out in the open, talk about it, solve it, and go on with life.*

7. *Blowing Up*

A fool gives full vent to his anger,
   but a wise man keeps himself under control
(Proverbs 29:11).

Anger is a dangerous emotion. Losing our temper, flying off the handle, and erupting into a volcanic rage is a serious and grave matter. How many times have we wished we could have reached out and seized our angry words before they struck their mark? How many times have we had to apologize for the wounds we have inflicted?

Angry people usually do not realize how deeply their sin hurts the other person. For us, it is only an emotional outburst, a chance to let off some steam; we feel better after we have said our piece. But for your husband or wife, the harsh words leave behind wounds—wounds like hurt, bitterness and fear that can cripple his or her ability to trust and feel close to you.

Some of us excuse ourselves with "Well, I do have a bit of a temper. It runs in my family, you know." Others of us are genuinely sorry, but feel enslaved to our anger. Still others of us use anger as a tool to intimidate, bully and get our way.

Jesus was angry only when God's honor was at stake or when the rights of the weak were being trampled upon. When he or his reputation was attacked, he remained poised and in control of his emotions. He did not allow himself to become peeved and irritated by the petty frustrations of life. If we are to be his disciples, we must imitate his example of patience in dealing with others.

8. Grumbling, Griping and Complaining

> Do everything without complaining or arguing, so that you may become blameless and pure, children of God without fault in a crooked and depraved generation, in which you shine like stars in the universe (Philippians 2:14-15).

It is unpleasant to talk to someone who always complains. To continually complain about life—how unfair, how rotten, how difficult—can quite effectively drive our beloved away from us. Griping, like many other communication problems, is actually a deep-seated character flaw to which we are often blind. If we knew how unattractive it is (even though others sometimes join us in our griping) we would retreat from such talk with horror. Perhaps it will take a marriage partner or another person to help us see the ugliness of this awful habit. When they point it out we need to listen. They are speaking truth we need to hear.

It is an especially great mistake to "dump" the difficulties of our day upon our spouses as soon as we see them or to call attention to something that has not been done right. It is far better to greet each other warmly, express gladness at seeing one another, and share some good news before we bring up the negative.

A right relationship with God brings gratitude, and this attitude will spill over into our marriages. When grumbling and griping are the rule, it shows not the faults of a spouse so much as a serious weakness in our relationship with God.

9. Lying

> Truthful lips endure forever,
>   but a lying tongue lasts only a moment
> (Proverbs 12:19).

We can have no relationship with anyone to whom we lie. Our spouses cannot be close to us, nor we to them, if there is deceit of *any* sort between us. We may believe that we have gotten away with our deception, but it still separates us. Down in our hearts we know that he or she does not truly know us. There is a phoniness and a falsehood about us. We can begin to feel insecure and unloved. We wonder, "If they *really* knew me, would they still *really* love me?" Loving the truth is the fundamental building block of character, and telling the truth is an essential step we take in building relationships with others. If we are to be close, our spouses must be able to trust our word absolutely.

Are you careless with the truth? Do you lie about anything—even "little" things? We may think that a minor fabrication is fine, but if we lie about anything—no matter how large or small—we have undercut our relationship. "Oh, the traffic was bad out there today," we say to mask our lack of discipline and consideration if we are late. "I don't remember you telling me that," we lamely offer to cover up our neglect.

The best policy is to simply tell the truth—even if it makes us look bad. "Simply let your 'Yes' be 'Yes,' and your 'No,' 'No'; anything beyond this comes from the evil one" (Matthew 5:37). The trust built on truth is far more important than a temporary saving of face you gain by lying. You don't ever really get away with it—lies and lying are always ultimately exposed. The rewards of truthfulness and the punishment for lying are written into the nature of the universe by our Creator!

I want my wife to be able to absolutely trust my words. I

want her to have total confidence in me. The payoff is a relationship at peace. There will be tough moments because of having to face my sins and weaknesses, but lying, which destroys the very fabric of our relationship, will simply have no place in our marriage.

10. Distractions

By distractions I mean the clamorous telephone, the ubiquitous TV, the intriguing Internet, the blaring radio and the isolating headset. All of these high-tech conveniences can prevent us from real and relaxing communication with our spouses. A host of other seemingly legitimate distractions such as our children, friends and busy schedules can keep us apart in spite of our intentions.

Radical steps must be taken to protect our relationships from all these competing intrusions. I remember in my early years of marriage developing the bad habit of watching reruns of one of my favorite television shows during dinner. I had some juicy rationalizations: We could talk at other times; I had worked hard all day and needed to unwind; the dinner hour was the only time this great program came on—all these excuses made perfect sense to me. Geri finally told me how she felt and what she thought (she is a great communicator!): Dinner should be a relaxed occasion when we share a meal and spend the hour conversing. She was right. I made a decision. A simple flick of the power switch to the left resolved the problem, and our marriage went on to glory!

Now we know what *not* to do. But just reading through this list will not change your marriage. You must take these things seriously. You must treat them as a threat to your relationship and make sure they are put out of your life.

This, however, is just half of the story. The other half is much more positive. How can a husband and wife create a relationship with great communication? What can be done to start it up and keep it going? How can we talk like never before?

How to Build Communication

1. *Seek to Synchronize*

Communication is an all-the-time thing, not just something we do in times of crisis. Too many of us get out of tune with our spouses and wait for problems to force us back into harmony. Instead, we should develop an ease and constancy of conversation that is rhythmic and instinctive.

How can we develop this kind of daily dialogue? Work at it all the time, every day: Talk as you dress for work or church, as you drive together, at mealtimes and during other regular activities. Much good can be done during "coffee time" or any time when we can get a few minutes during the day. Such times form the fabric of a great marriage.

2. *Spend Special Seasons*

In addition to daily times conversing, we need to regularly carve out larger blocks of time to spend together. Take walks or go bike riding with one another. Get the kids to bed early and spend a quiet evening alone at home. Busy schedules make this a challenge, but we strongly urge that you retire for the evening at the same time. This provides a natural opportunity to wrap things up by spending a few minutes catching up on the day's events—this can also lead to other exciting forms of communication as well! Get away together overnight. You don't have to wait until anniversaries or birthdays—just pack a bag and go! It doesn't take a huge amount of planning or money to spend an evening at a nearby hotel or bed and breakfast. And even one night away can seem much longer when you learn to relax and enjoy yourselves. Every now and then we hear of couples with teenagers who haven't done this since the kids were born! They would be in a lot better shape to take care of those kids if they would get away once in a while. What kids need most is a mom and a dad with a great relationship.

Shortly after our first two children were born, Geri and I realized we were seeing less of each other. There didn't seem to be enough of us to go around. Time became scarce, conversations were interrupted, and our marriage began to

suffer. We solved this dilemma by getting a baby-sitter to watch the kids so we could go out for breakfast on Saturdays. As the kids grew up and their weekend sports leagues began to intrude on our breakfast, we changed it to a lunch date on Mondays. What began as a weekly highlight has now become a pillar in our marriage. Today, with four children and a much more complicated and busy life, this weekly time is an absolute necessity not only for our relationship's sake but for keeping our entire family organized and together.

3. Be Refreshingly Real

In his book *The Friendship Factor* Alan Loy McGinnis observes,

> Studies show, to no one's surprise, that newly married couples talk to each other more than twice as much as couples married for years. But the content of their talk is even more telling than the amount. At first, it is the sort of talk that close friends enjoy–the subjective exploring and mutual revealing of beliefs and feelings, likes and dislikes, and the trading and comparing of ideas about sex, aesthetic subjects, and plans for the future. Later the talk is more mundane–decisions about money, household matters, problems with the children.[1]

To have a friendship, couples must talk heart-to-heart. When we lose the deep bonding of our souls, marriage becomes stale, empty and lifeless. We may perform a daily routine, but that's all it is—a performance—there is little or no satisfying intimacy and friendship. Somewhere along the way we become superficial. We no longer talk with each other; we merely exchange information. And when we reach this point, both of us are prime candidates for adultery.

I once counseled a couple whose relationship vividly illustrates this problem. They were married for more than ten years, had three beautiful children and appeared to have a great life. But they neglected each other. They never learned how to talk deeply with one other. They abused drugs. They lied to each other. They continued on this path until both became unfaithful. As the woman tearfully confessed to her

adultery, she said to her husband, "So many times I just wanted to talk to you—*and you weren't there for me.*"

By the grace and power of God, this story ended happily. The couple surrendered their lives to God and found the strength to be open, to forgive each other and to rekindle their love. But others have yet to learn this lesson. You need to decide that you will not be another tragic statistic—that you will begin *now* to be honest and real with each other.

4. Learn the Levels

In the book quoted earlier, McGinnis points out that there are three levels of communication: facts, opinions and emotions.[2] To have a close marriage, it is imperative that we learn to communicate truthfully and openly on all three levels. To help understand this, consider this scenario:

Fact: Husband is late for a lunch date with his wife.

His opinion: "This is my secretary's fault. She always hits me with something just when I'm ready to leave. But, I still might have made it on time if I hadn't stopped at that stupid newsstand on the way to the car."

Her opinion: "Late again! He could have left work sooner if he really wanted to. He just takes me for granted. This is just another example of his lack of love and consideration for me. And he's not even going to listen to me if I try to tell him how I feel. I wonder if he even loves me anymore. Oh, maybe it is all my fault—I'm always nagging him about something."

His emotions: (1) anger at his secretary (2) anxiety about his wife's possible reaction and (3) guilt brought on by his opinion that he could have been on time.

Her emotions: (1) anger (2) hurt (3) hopelessness caused by her opinion that he will not listen to her (4) fear that he does not really love her anymore and (5) guilt caused by her opinion that she may be too critical of him.

Are you as lost as I am on all this? Is it any wonder that the simplest of human events can become so terribly complex and that a minor problem can erupt into a major crisis?

Many situations become more difficult because men and women usually communicate on different levels. *Facts* and *opinions* are paramount to a man; whereas *emotions* and *opin-*

ions are vital to a woman. "Can't we just stick to the facts?" protests the husband. "Why are you so unfeeling?" replies the wife. To argue this way is futile—it is attacking the person, not the root problem. Instead, we need to work with our spouses. We should recognize and understand on which level they are communicating and then help them to understand where we are. When we do, we are on our way to a marriage blessed with outstanding communication. (We will address the issue of resolving conflict in further detail in Chapter 9.)

5. Lighten Up

Many of you believe that anything to do with communication is by nature negative. In your minds it always means dealing with something difficult, tedious, unpleasant and hard. No wonder you dread anything akin to deep conversation! Or, if you are the "heavy," this is why your spouse groans whenever you want to "have a talk." Others believe that having any sort of meaningful discussion requires a minimum of three hours in an isolated, perfect environment. Such thinking is foolish and unrealistic, and only produces frustration in others.

"Deep" doesn't have to be draining or depressing. Honesty is far more than just gut-wrenching confessions or an exploration of the dark side of your soul. Communication goes beyond talking about problems, disagreements and unpleasant experiences. It also means expressing our love, our appreciation and our respect for each other. It includes sharing the good news and good things in life with each other. Enjoy some laughter, share some memories, talk about your dreams, share your hearts...and lighten up!

6. Speak Silently

Words, phrases and sentences form only a small part of how we communicate. We convey much more with our attention, our expressions, our tone of voice and our touch.

Attention. Gaze at your spouses when you talk to them. Give them your complete attention. Look into their eyes— not just in their general direction. This lets them know you are listening and care. It is frustrating to speak to someone who is preoccupied—reading the paper, staring at the TV, stir-

ring something in a pot, or drifting away in thought. If the conversation is light, then we can afford to listen as we go about doing something else, but we must be sensitive as to when to stop what we are doing and give our full attention to our spouses.

Expression. Look at your spouse with a warm, friendly expression. Be like Jesus, who could communicate his love to a complete stranger with the look on his face: "Jesus looked at him and loved him " (Mark 10:21). A blank stare communicates boredom. The tight-knitted brow conveys preoccupation or weariness in listening. The sarcastic sneer indicates disrespect. Need I go on? Get your heart into the conversation and a good expression on your face!

Tone. The same words spoken in different tones can have different meanings and different effects. This is the place so many of us stumble in our communication skills. Our words may be harmless, but our manner is harmful. Many of us use harsh tones—some out of habit, others with deadly intent. Still others moan, groan, drone and whine. Turn on a tape recorder, leave it hidden in a busy room in your home, forget it is on, and play it back later. You may be shocked at what you hear. The tape only records the truth—so if your tone is offensive, change it! Learn to speak with a pleasant, positive intonation to your voice. "Pleasant words are a honeycomb, sweet to the soul and healing to the bones" (Proverbs 16:24).

Touch. Jesus frequently touched people. He was not distant and aloof: He had physical contact with individuals in every conceivable situation. He touched the deformed leper whom he could have healed from afar: "Filled with compassion, Jesus reached out his hand and touched the man" (Mark 1:41). He took the children in his arms to bless them (Mark 10:16). These and many other examples show how Jesus understood the value of the human touch in communicating with all kinds of people.

Since we who are married are "one flesh," we ought to touch freely and frequently. A marriage with little or no touching is not a close marriage. Hold hands. Snuggle up close. Give a little squeeze on the shoulder as you walk by. Sit or

stand next to each other in public. Give a relaxing neck or shoulder rub after a long day. Hug and kiss in greeting, or for no particular reason at all!

An acquaintance of mine tells a story that happened after his father's death. He walked up behind his elderly mother as she was doing the dishes and began to rub her shoulders. She immediately began to cry. She turned to him and said, "I'm sorry, but since your father died, it has been very long since anyone has touched me." We need to be touched. It heals hurts and pains, it comforts and moves hearts in ways we do not understand. So go ahead and touch—and unleash its mystical, uniting power in your marriage!

7. Show Common Courtesy

> Life is not lost by dying! Life is lost
> Minute by minute, day by dragging day,
> In all the thousand, small, uncaring ways.
> *Stephen Vincent Benét*

Little things make a big difference. Life does not consist exclusively of great events—it is made up of a myriad of small, seemingly unnoticed moments. Often it is not the one big injury that ruins a marriage—it is the accumulation of small hurts and discourtesies over time. Solomon said it long ago: "Catch for us the foxes, the little foxes that ruin the vineyards, our vineyards that are in bloom" (Song of Songs 2:15). Let me suggest some ways to catch the "little foxes" of discourtesy:

Express appreciation. Say "thank you" for the routine services your spouse performs in the course of the day. Express gratitude for preparing a meal, folding the clothes, mowing the lawn, taking care of the finances or running an errand. Such thankfulness is the oil that makes the machinery of marriage run smoothly.

Do small, unexpected favors. A little act of kindness, showing some extra attention to our spouses, says "I love you" in ways that words do not. Many times after I have had a stressful day my wife will present me with my favorite candy bar. It doesn't solve the problems, but it makes me feel a whole lot better—and it only costs a few cents! Some mornings I will pour Geri a cup of coffee, fix it just the way she likes and take it up to her as she is getting dressed. A smile spreads across her face and she responds by saying something like, "Thank you, thank you, you wonderful husband." If this sounds a little hokey to you, I say, don't knock it 'til you've tried it!

Lighten the load. Take on a task that your mate usually performs. Stop by and pick up the kids from school. Volunteer to run a bothersome errand. Make the phone call that has been nagging him or her all day. Clean out a closet. Wash the car. Hang a picture. Paint a room. Balance the checkbook. Do something to make his or her life less pressured and hectic.

Compliment appearance. Husband, tell your wife when she looks nice. Don't speak up only when you are displeased, dummy! Compliment her even when she is not dressed in her very best outfit—give her credit for looking attractive anytime. Don't wait for her to ask how she looks—go ahead and praise her without prompting—she'll be more likely to believe you then! Wife, give your husband those compliments, too. He needs and appreciates them even if he is too proud to admit it.

8. Share the Spiritual

> "For where two or three come together in my name, there am I with them" (Matthew 18:20).

Our relationship with God is the strongest bond of unity in marriage. The couple that spends time together in prayer and Bible study will be close—far closer than they ever dreamed!

Devote a set time during the week for spiritual discussion and prayer. Pray together frequently throughout the week. Husbands, take your leadership seriously. Make sure these times happen. Be the initiator. Geri and I pray before we retire for the evening. It is usually brief, but it is very important to us. (It is hard to go to bed angry at one another when you end the day with prayer!) We also pray at meals and before we go into meetings, appointments or social engagements.

We make every effort to follow Paul's admonition to "pray continually," (1 Thessalonians 5:17) and we find it to be a great and unifying experience. It keeps us close to God and to one another.

Help each other spiritually. Share encouraging verses from your own study of the Scriptures. (When was the last time you did this?) If you are struggling, open up to your spouse. If your partner is undergoing a spiritual challenge, discuss how to overcome it. Speak up. Encourage, urge, admonish—whatever is appropriate for the need of the hour, do it!

9. Practice the Praise Principle

> Finally, brothers, whatever is true, whatever is noble, whatever is right, whatever is pure, whatever is lovely, whatever is admirable—if anything is excellent or praiseworthy—think about such things (Philippians 4:8).

Focus your thoughts on the good qualities in your spouse. If you occupy yourself with the pure, the lovely, the admirable, the excellent and the praiseworthy characteristics in your mate, then you, and they, will reap a benefit.

It has been observed that it takes five compliments to offset the effect of one criticism. When you give compliments, watch your spouse—and your marriage—blossom before your eyes. Say the words of love and praise. Speak them frequently, fearlessly, warmly and sincerely. Don't hold back! Can't think of anything nice to say? You married this person for their great qualities. Make a list of those traits, and read it every day for a month. Stop focusing on their weaknesses and faults!

Write down your feelings of love, thanksgiving and affection in cards and notes. Some of us who stumble over the spoken word wax eloquent when we write. Use occasions like birthdays and anniversaries to capture your feelings on a card. Surprise him or her with a note scrawled on a scrap of paper and left taped on the mirror, tucked under the pillow, or stashed away in a briefcase or a purse. These are small, thoughtful expressions that make marriage a joy and can rekindle a dying love.

10. Faithfully Forgive

> Bear with each other and forgive whatever grievances you
> may have against one another. Forgive as the Lord forgave
> you (Colossians 3:13).

If you are feeling a bit guilty and frustrated right now, it is understandable. The challenges in communication can be overwhelming. As we realize the many ways we have failed and the weaknesses in our character that have brought those failures about, we can want to pretend they aren't there or just give up in despair.

That is where forgiveness comes in. Frequently in marriage we say the wrong thing (or fail to say the right thing!). As James wrote: "All kinds of animals, birds, reptiles and creatures of the sea are being tamed and have been tamed by man, but no man can tame the tongue. It is a restless evil, full of deadly poison" (James 3:7-8). We will have to be forgiven and ask their forgiveness repeatedly. How much will we have to forgive? Peter once asked Jesus this question and suggested that seven might be the limit. Jesus replied "'I tell you not seven times, but seventy-seven times'" (Matthew 18:22). I think Jesus is saying to us that our forgiveness in life (and especially in marriage) will have to be as generous and faithful as God's. We must forgive again and again. And we must express it freely when we do.

These are the basics on communication. Understand them. Work on them. Master them. Communication takes work and commitment. Those who are lazy will have no success. But when you care enough to communicate, you help your wife or husband feel your love. Listen to Paul's great statement about love in 1 Corinthians 13 and notice how so much that he says is directly related to communication and the principles we have talked about in this chapter:

Love is patient, love is kind. It does not envy, it does not boast, it is not proud. It is not rude, it is not self-seeking, it is not easily angered, it keeps no record of wrongs. Love does not delight in evil but rejoices with the truth. It always protects, always trusts, always hopes, always perseveres (1 Corinthians 13:4-7).

If you don't communicate, you don't love. If you don't embrace these qualities of love, you will never communicate. According to a best-selling book, men seem to be from one planet and women from another, but God has a plan for us to share our lives with one another, and his plan will produce rich and rewarding results.

CHAPTER 3

When a Man Loves a Woman

For the husband is the head of the
wife as Christ is the head of the
church....Husbands, love your wives,
just as Christ loved the church....

EPHESIANS 5:23, 25

My family once owned a beautiful, huge Chow dog named Bruno. With his thick, shaggy, rust-colored mane he looked like a cross between a lion and a bear. He had a powerful, stocky build and the trademark blue-black tongue of the breed. Since we lived in Florida, in the summer months we would often have those late afternoon rain showers that would hit quickly and intensely, and then, just as quickly, go away. Bruno had an interesting habit: He would stand out in the back yard during these downpours as if it were perfectly sunny, strutting around the yard as usual and seemingly oblivious to the torrential rain. We had another dog, a mixed breed named Buster, who had a lot more sense. When the rains came, he would retreat into the garage. Buster would then look curiously (as did I and my family) at his yardmate standing out in the rain.

Later I noticed another interesting phenomenon about Bruno. Several hours after one of these rainstorms had come and gone he would suddenly look around, shake himself, and run to seek shelter in the garage. He would stay there for quite some time, staring out at the yard as if it were raining. Perplexed, I pondered this for a while and then I realized the reason behind this strange behavior. Bruno *saw* the rain, but he didn't *feel* it right away. His coat was so thick it took several hours for the moisture to penetrate it and reach his skin. It took him much more time to figure out what was going on.

It was later that I applied the Bruno Principle to the human world and to the male gender specifically. It can be put this way: *Men don't get it.* They are not naturally sensitive. They can go for hours or days in the midst of a downpour in their wife's life and not grasp or feel what is happening to her. They wander around thinking everything is fine when it is not. It ought to be as plain as the nose on their face, but it isn't. Suddenly, eventually, they will wake up and feel what is really happening. They will then react, but it may be too late. The storm may already be over. If men are going to become sensitive, it will take learning some new skills.

Men, we don't have to be a *Bruno!* Yes, we must be strong, powerful and confident, and yes, we need to be tough and firm—but we must be loving and sensitive, as well. If we are to be mature men, if we are to be genuinely masculine, there must be a better way.

So how does a man go about being a husband? Is there a manual he can turn to and look up exactly what he needs to know in any situation? Is there a list of rules he can follow that will make him the husband he should be?

The Bible's emphasis is not on rules but on a role model. It does not provide some*thing* to do, but rather some*one* to imitate. There is a marriage relationship in which the husband is the perfect example. A man can look at this husband and be completely confident in imitating his life and example. Who is this husband? *Jesus.* Who is his wife? *The church.*

The relationship between Jesus and the church is the pattern that God wants men to follow in building a marriage. God does not lay out many specific rules—"if this happens, do this" kinds of statements. Marriage is simply too large and dynamic an enterprise to be reduced to a set of rules. Instead, men are shown an *attitude* to possess and a *model* to imitate. And Jesus possesses that attitude and is that model.

God gives husbands this challenge: Be like Jesus in the way you treat your wife. In any situation that arises in his marriage, the husband is to ask himself, "What would Jesus do?" Jesus' relationship to the church can be summed up in two great concepts: He *leads* her, and he *loves* her.

The Husband As Leader

There is a great deal of confusion today about the concept of the husband's leadership in marriage. It is critical that we address it. I urge you to open your mind and your eyes to what God has to say about this crucial and difficult subject.

The Bible teaches that "the husband is the head of the wife" (Ephesians 5:23). As such, he has the role of leader in the marriage relationship. That men are to lead is not merely social convention—it is intrinsic to the very nature of creation:

> Now I want you to realize that the head of every man is Christ, and the head of the woman is man, and the head of Christ is God (1 Corinthians 11:3).

This principle is made even more clear by the charge given to wives to "submit to your husbands as to the Lord" (Ephesians 5:22). God has ordered and arranged marriage so that men are to be the leaders of their wives. This is the clear and unmistakable teaching of the Bible.

You, as the husband, are in charge. It is neither arrogant nor presumptuous of you to lead. It is wrong for you not to lead. Marriage is a partnership, to be sure, but the husband is the senior partner, put in that position by God. The husband must be a leader who will listen, weigh and consider but who he has the charge, challenge and accountability for the final decision. There is a time for the husband to give up his rights and wishes and submit to his wife, but he must never do so out of weakness, nor must he surrender his position as leader.

Many husbands have abandoned their leadership role. They are aloof and alone. They are too preoccupied, busy and distracted to assume their God-given responsibility. Others are weak and intimidated. Perhaps a wife's assertive, aggressive personality has beaten a man down, or it may be that she feels she must act in this manner to compensate for the void he has created by his lack of confidence. It could be that our culture with its humanistic attitudes and overreaction to male injustices has stripped some of us of our conviction. Others of us may be depressed and discouraged. As we have gotten older, the difficulties of life have wearied us and lessened our motivation to try anymore. Some of us have withdrawn from leading because we are cynical, angry and bitter. Others of us are afraid of our own heavy-handedness. Perhaps we saw our fathers mistreat our mothers, or we recall with shame our own harshness, and in backing away from these mistakes, we have backed out of leading altogether.

None of these is the appropriate response. When circumstances are challenging, God does not throw out the plan; he makes a better man! God is not so much concerned with the *position* of leadership as with the *heart* of the leader. He gives the position, and then teaches us how to go about filling it. The right model and the right motive will produce the right method. The model is Jesus. His motive is love.

The Husband As Lover

Husbands, we are challenged to love our wives with the greatest love that has ever been shown—the love of Christ for his church. More than anything else we do for our wives, we are to love them. We must love them with all of our being, all of our heart and all of our passion. The only love that is to surpass our love for our wives is our love for God himself. In this definitive passage for husbands, Paul describes several specific ways we are to love:

> Husbands, love your wives, just as Christ loved the church and gave himself up for her to make her holy, cleansing her by the washing with water through the word, and to present her to himself as a radiant church, without stain or wrinkle or any other blemish, but holy and blameless. In this same way, husbands ought to love their wives as their own bodies. He who loves his wife loves himself. After all, no one ever hated his own body, but he feeds and cares for it, just as Christ does the church—for we are members of his body. "For this reason a man will leave his father and mother and be united to his wife, and the two will become one flesh." This is a profound mystery–but I am talking about Christ and the church. However, each one of you also must love his wife as he loves himself, and the wife must respect her husband (Ephesians 5:25-33).

An Unselfish Love

So great was his love for his church that Jesus "gave himself up for her" (Ephesians 5:25). He loved the church enough to die for her. He willingly endured privation, abuse, ridicule, suffering, pain and torture for his bride, the church. He gave up his own will that she might be saved. Throughout his life he willingly laid himself aside that he might serve her and save her. Any leadership he exercised was not for the purpose of glorying in his power or in gaining personal benefit; his leadership was for the blessing and benefit of his bride. Aside from sinning against God himself, there was nothing Jesus would not do to demonstrate and prove his love and win the heart of his bride.

As husbands, we must sacrifice ourselves for our wives in a number of specific ways. We must give up our *time*. A man must be willing to give up what he would like to do to meet his wife's needs and spend time with her. If we are unwilling to do this, how can we say, and how can they feel, that we deeply love them? We must give of our *energy*. It takes expenditure of vast quantities of physical and emotional strength to love. Jesus gave unstintingly of himself. He was so weary that he could sleep his way through a life-threatening storm (Mark 4:35-39) and so exhausted that he finally collapsed beneath the weight of his cross—but still he loved. As disciples of Jesus we have a number of needs crying out for our attention. We can feel pulled in a lot of directions. There are children to love and Christians to serve. Then there are the poor and the lost, but our wives *must not* get the leftovers. God will bless you when you put your wife's needs above all others, giving you strength to help her and others. How much pure effort are you expending to show your wife your love? We must give up our *wishes and desires*. Jesus did not come to be served but to serve and to give his life (Matthew 20:25-28). A man who has to have everything his way is not loving his wife.

Jesus knew he was the Lord of his church, but he humbled himself to serve, to do the unpleasant, menial task of foot-washing (John 13:1-17). He challenged us: "Now that I, your Lord and Teacher, have washed your feet, you also should wash one another's feet" (John 13:14). A man must learn how to love and serve his wife, and yet retain his role of leadership. Jesus did not give his bride her way if it meant surrendering to her petty selfishness or undermining her obedience to God—that would have been weakness and compromise. But he willingly gave up his pleasures and comforts to meet her needs, and that is what husbands also must do.

A Sensitive Love

Paul wrote that "husbands ought to love their wives as their own bodies" (Ephesians 5: 28). This passage describes a special kind of love husbands should have—a sensitive love. Wives must be loved with a profound degree of feeling. Since we are one flesh (Ephesians 5:31) we must treat our wives as if they were part of our own bodies.

Men are notoriously insensitive. Why else are we told firmly and repeatedly to be sensitive unless it does not come easy for us? If there is any time when I see the pain of wives the most, it is when their feelings are not understood or considered by their husbands. The hurt can be etched deeply in a woman's eyes, or it may come out as a hard edge of cynicism and bitter wit, but it is unmistakable and widespread. I hurt for women who live with unfeeling, insensitive husbands. The woman who is married to a kind, gentle and loving husband shows it. Jesus' goal is for his church to be "radiant" (Ephesians 5: 27). The original language carries the idea that she is meant to be "glorious." If Jesus' goal for his bride is that she be radiant and glorious, then our goal for our wives should be the same. A wife should have a sparkle in her eyes, a confidence to her bearing and a joyfulness in her smile. Radiance and joy need to flow out of her and be instinctive, unstudied and unbridled. She will be confident, yet without arrogance or conceit, because she is deeply secure in her husband's nurturing love.

Husbands, we are taught to love our wives as our own bodies. We are to be as sensitive to our mates' needs—whatever they may be—as we are to our own physical needs. There are two words used to describe this love in Ephesians 5:29. The first (translated "feeds") conveys the meaning of nourishing a child to maturity: being certain that it has the proper feeding to bring it to fullness of stature. The second (translated "cares for") conveys the concept of "cherishing": showing tender love and affection. These terms describe the kind of sensitive love men should have. As we are aware of the needs of our own bodies and respond to them, so we should be aware and solicitous of the needs of our wives. Jesus does not love his church distantly and unemotionally. He feels for her and feels with her. His is not a compromising or superficial love, but a compassionate, tender love. He experiences deep feelings and emotions for his bride.

Husbands should be sensitive to the *emotional* needs of their wives. Is she discouraged? Is she lonely? Is she frustrated? As a husband, you should be aware of any feelings of this nature. You should not be slow to realize these situations—you ought to know your wife so well and care for her so much that you can pick up on her needs immediately and instinctively, without always having to be told.

We should be sensitive to our wives' *physical* needs. Is she tired? Weary? Sick? Does she have any physical discomfort at all? Peter says that women are the "weaker partner" (1 Peter 3:7). This is a simple reference to the fact that normally women are not as physically strong as men. This has nothing to do with superiority or inferiority, but with simple biological fact. Men are often unsympathetic to their wives' lesser physical stamina and strength. If she is weary and tired, we should step in and help her get some rest. If she is ill, we ought to help her get well.

Men, let's be honest—we pamper ourselves when we get sick. The house becomes a hospital when we are ill! Our wives are sent scurrying to buy medicines, to make chicken soup and to keep things quiet. "Tell that cat to stop stomping through the living room!" shouts the Infirm Male from his bedroom sanctuary. But when our wives get sick? "Oh honey, just vacuum the house, cook dinner and keep going to work. You'll sweat that fever right out." And we wonder why there is a Women's Lib Movement!

We must also be sensitive to our wives' *social* needs. Women often feel stifled socially because they feel as if their entire lives revolve around their husbands and children. In one sense, this is true for both wives and for husbands—the most significant relationships in terms of time and emotional investment are those of our own household. But we cannot limit ourselves, or our wives, to these few social contacts. As wonderful as you are, husband, you are not enough. And as cute and special as our kids are, they are not enough, either. Women need contact with other adult friends outside the family circle. We need to have relationships with other couples with whom we can go out and have fun. We need people we can kick back with, laugh with, relax with and enjoy adult conversation with. Women also need friendships with other women. It is a good and healthy thing, and you should encourage and help her have time to go out with her female friends. These companions cannot and must not take your place (or that of your children) in your wife's heart, but they are an essential part of her life, and you do her a grave disservice if you do not encourage her to meet this vital social need.

We must be sensitive to our wives' *spiritual* needs. A woman's relationship with God and her spiritual life must be encouraged by you, as her husband, more than by anyone else. You should pray with her and discuss spiritual subjects with her. You should encourage and lead her to put God first and to grow spiritually. You should encourage her to spend daily time in prayer and study of the Bible (and if need be, help with the kids to give her some privacy). When you see your wife faltering or weakening spiritually, you should be concerned and helpful, not waiting for someone else to step in. Sadly, it is my experience that it is usually the wife who is more spiritually sensitive than her husband. Somehow men have gotten the idea that spirituality is a "woman thing." The classic picture is that of a wife pleading with her reluctant husband to go to church and have concern for spiritual values. God's plan is for the man to lead the way in this area and to love his wife enough to challenge her by word and deed to be strong in the faith.

An Exclusive Love

"'For this reason a man will leave his father and mother and be united to his wife, and the two will become one flesh'" (Ephesians 5:31). Our love for our wives is to be our greatest human love. Our wives must occupy first place in our hearts. Only God himself is to have a greater devotion. Only with our wives are we "one flesh." We are one person. There is no other relationship like it, and therefore no greater human love. Our loyalty and love for our wives must be greater than our loyalty to our parents. We are to leave them and build a life with our wives.

Some of us have not placed our wives in this unique position. We have other loves that are greater. Perhaps it is our love for our mothers and/or fathers. This will be evidenced by a greater loyalty to them than to our wives. We allow them to criticize and distance us from our wives. We allow them to dictate the priorities of our lives. While we should always honor our mothers and fathers, our wives must come before them. This is a commitment we must make, one they should absolutely know and feel we have made. We cannot lessen our loyalty to our wives to please our parents. We cannot remain more emotionally tied to them than to our wives, nor can we remain dependent upon them. We must build a life together with our wives, with its foundation based upon Christ.

For others of us, our jobs take first place. When the job calls, we jump, even if it means harming our marriage. There is a place for sacrifice in doing our job and being a good employee, but no career should ever be allowed to come above our wives (or our children.) No amount of money, prestige or personal fulfillment should make us neglect our wives.

Certainly, another woman should never have any place in our hearts or our interest. A man with any tendency in this direction must deal with it decisively by getting open with God and another male friend who holds to God's standard. Our wives should know beyond any shadow of a doubt where they stand with us. A wife should be totally confident that she is number one and no one else is even close! When she knows this, you will have the foundation upon which you can build a great marriage.

An Initiating Love

"Husbands, love your wives just as Christ loved the church" (Ephesians 5:25). I have always been struck by how Jesus loved us first. He initiated, loving us before we loved him, and he cared about us before we cared for him. If Jesus had waited for the church to love him first, he would still be waiting! Our love for Jesus is a "because" love: "We love *because* he first loved us" (1 John 4:19, emphasis added). Our relationship with Jesus began by his loving us first and is sustained by his continuing to love us. He is the initiator, we are responders.

During courtship, men are usually the initiators. Even if the woman is the first to be interested, somewhere along the way the man has to start taking the lead. Once we are married, this pattern must continue, or the marriage will suffer. The wife will especially suffer. She will continually bear the uncertainty of wondering how her husband feels about her and will be insecure. Being in the role of follower, she wants to be loved and protected. If this reassurance is not there, she will feel inadequate and unworthy. Or, she may begin to look for love from some source other than her husband: her children, her parents, her job, her friends or another man.

Men, we should be the initiators of love. Years into our marriages, we should *still* be the aggressive givers of love and assurance to our wives. We must never back away from showing our love in words and deeds. We should be a fountainhead of love for our wives. Many times I have heard men say that their wives and children do not love and appreciate them. My answer to this complaint is this: If you pour out love in generous measure, you will be loved in return. Your wife will be utterly devoted to you, because you love her as no one else does. And the same will be true of your children.

Take the initiative. Show her you love her. Write cards, give gifts and take her out to special places. Be a gentleman. Show extraordinary courtesy and consideration. Say the words of love. Do not wait for her to make the first move. In this way you imitate Jesus, who initiates love to his church and continues to win her heart by his continued love, attention and sustenance.

A Love Without Bitterness

"Husbands, love your wives and do not be harsh with them" (Colossians 3:19). The word translated "harsh" in the above verse has as its base meaning "to make bitter." It is the same root word used in Hebrews 12:15 to refer to the "bitter root." A good translation could also be, "Husbands, love your wives and do not be embittered against them." The verse is an admonition to husbands to not be embittered against or frustrated with their wives—to not be critical, nagging, angry men.

Husbands, ask yourselves, *Am I bitter toward my wife? Do I have a critical attitude? Do I make her feel she can never do anything right?* If you are bitter against her, she may feel the same way about you, so ask yourself another question: *Is my wife radiantly happy, or is she bitter?* If she is bitter, then take a look in the mirror, and ask yourself if it is your fault. She is in the role of follower. If you, as her leader, do not treat her with love, you may drive her to bitterness. Think about it from your own perspective: If you served under an employer who was constantly critical, harsh and unfair and who continually nagged you about your performance on the job, how would you feel? If you are uncaring and overbearing toward your wife, you make her feel the same way. Some of us who have been so free to blame our wives' bitterness on their lack of spirituality and ingratitude need to take responsibility for our part in their problem. A husband can go a long way toward making his wife's life a joyful and more spiritual one by his tender concern.

A woman was once asked by a friend "Do you wake up grouchy every morning?" To this she replied, "No, sometimes I just let him sleep!" I am reminded of another story about a woman who lived with a harsh, critical husband. She decided she would treat him kindly even though he was difficult to live with. One morning she made his favorite breakfast: scrambled eggs, toast, bacon, orange juice and coffee. She placed it on a beautiful platter with flowers and the morning newspaper and took it up to him so that he could have breakfast in bed. He scowled and said gruffly, "I didn't want scrambled eggs. I wanted fried eggs." With a smile she said, "I'm sorry, dear." The next morning she tried again—this time with fried eggs. When presented with his beautiful breakfast tray, the husband said, "Today I wanted scrambled eggs." Undaunted, the woman said to herself. "I know what I'll do. I'll scramble one egg and fry the other." The next morning, she took up his platter with one scrambled and one fried egg. The husband looked at her with his typical frown and said, "*You scrambled the wrong egg!*" Husbands, I hope we are not this bad off!

A Considerate Love

> Husbands, in the same way be considerate as you live with your wives, and treat them with respect as the weaker partner and as heirs with you of the gracious gift of life, so that nothing will hinder your prayers (1 Peter 3:7).

Peter tells us we should be considerate of our wives. The literal translation of this phrase is "live together with understanding." To love our wives is to be understanding of their nature. We should treat them like women, not like men. We should treat them as our wives and not as employees or as our personal servants. So many of us men understand neither our wives' feminine nature nor their role as followers. God has designed their feminine nature to thrive when given our love and attention, and in their role as followers, they need our consideration.

Second, Peter says we should treat our wives with respect. A more literal translation is "showing honor." This means that in private and in public, we should treat our wives with utmost respect. In private we should praise our wives for their great qualities and tell them continually how much we admire and appreciate them. We should hold up our wives before our children and families as women we revere and appreciate. In the presence of our friends, business associates and neighbors we should lift up our wives with praise and appreciation. We should do this when they are present and when they are absent. This kind of treatment causes a woman to blossom with high self-esteem. She also falls more deeply in love with her husband with every compliment he gives.

Third, Peter notes in this passage that our wives are joint heirs with us of the gracious gift of life. As men, we are the leaders, but we must remember that before God, our wives are our equals. *We are not superior.* Sometimes, we feel because we are in the role of leadership it means we are better than our wives. Nothing could be further from the truth. It has been my privilege to serve as a leader in God's church for many years, and I can say that there are many people that I lead who are far more talented than I. Many of them have qualities of character that are superior to mine. I am their leader because I have the ability and talent to do it, not because I am innately superior. If I begin to feel that I am better than they are, I will become an arrogant, oppressive leader. Anyone, especially a wife, who is led by someone like this can lose heart, become discouraged and lose faith and confidence.

Fourth, Peter gives us a solemn warning in this passage. He says that if we do not treat our wives respectfully, God will not hear our prayers. God views disrespect for a wife as disrespect for him. God opposes oppressive, dictatorial leaders. He will ultimately judge them. This somber warning serves notice that God holds us who are husbands accountable for our treatment of our wives. We must strive with all of our hearts to love our wives in the way that Christ has loved his church.

To be effective husbands, we will have to excel in both the role of leader and of lover. We cannot choose one and reject the other. Unfortunately, that is what I see too many husbands doing.

Some of us want to be the strong, powerful leaders of our wives, but do not wish to love them in equal measure. We are decisive and forceful, but we lack the compassion and tenderness of Jesus. Our wives suffer for it. They look and feel beaten down and they lack confidence. We do not lead our wives; we drive and push them. We do not win their hearts; we defeat their wills. Our wives are not eager to please us; they are afraid to offend us. Jesus did not lead in this manner. The people who followed him were drawn to his Lordship by his love demonstrated by his death on the cross (John 12:32). If your wife reflects a spirit of discouragement, if she is not radiant, do not be quick to blame it on *her* insecurities, insubmissiveness, faithlessness and pride. Instead, take a hard look in the mirror, and ask yourself, "Am I loving my wife the way Jesus loved the church?"

Others of us want to love our wives, but not lead them. We are kind, caring and considerate but lack pathetically in masculine force and confidence. Perhaps we are timid by nature. Maybe we are lazy and simply do not want to make the effort to lead. Perhaps we have lost confidence due to past mistakes. Do not be too quick to blame your failures on your wife's aggressiveness—your weakness may be the root of the problem. Perhaps she needs to change, and there may be some difficult moments in helping her to see that need, but you must press forward. Most strong women I have dealt with in marriage counseling have, in spite of leaving the opposite impression, longed for their husbands to rise up and lead them. I have seen the hearts of many such "tough" women melt with gratitude when they realized that their husbands were going to begin providing dynamic, loving leadership in their marriage.

Whichever of these areas is your weakness, recognize it and change it. Be honest with yourself. Make a strong resolve that you, with God's help and the help of others, will be the husband who leads and loves his wife just as Jesus leads and loves his church.

CHAPTER 4

R-E-S-P-E-C-T

She brings him good, not harm,
all the days of her life.

PROVERBS 31:12

There are three great needs a man has of his wife. He needs her to respect him, to complement him and to love him.

Respect Him

...the wife must respect her husband (Ephesians 5:33).

What does it mean for a wife to respect her husband? It means she must honor him, revere him and appreciate him. In her heart she must value her husband as a man and as a person. He should know in his heart of hearts that this is the way she genuinely feels.

Wife, the Bible teaches you to respect your husband for two primary reasons. The first is because of his role of leadership in your marriage. Wives need to submit to their husbands as the church submits to her leader, Christ himself (Ephesians 5:22-24). Your husband has been given this role by God, and the only way leaders are able to effectively lead is if they are respected by those being led. The second reason you should respect your husband is because he *needs* it. As the wife must have the husband's love to feel complete and whole as a woman, the husband requires his wife's respect and admiration to feel fulfilled as a man. Without your respect, your husband will always sense a void in his soul—this is the way God made him.

If you do not deeply respect your husband, no matter what he may accomplish in life, he will not feel himself to be fully a man. In a practical sense, he cannot perform to the full measure of his talents unless he has your support and esteem. Many men whose wives do not respect them lose heart and sink into discouragement and depression. They feel like failures and become weaker as the years go by. Other men react differently. If they feel disrespect from their wives, they become more aggressive, domineering and controlling. Such men become harsh and critical as a means to force their wives "into line." Still other men seek fulfillment elsewhere to make up for what they do not receive from their wives. They become workaholics, immerse themselves in sports or distract themselves by involvement in causes and activities. They may seek to fill the void they feel by attempting to win respect from their coworkers, friends or, most tragically of all, by turning to sexual involvement with other women.

Many women want to be respectful of their husbands but find themselves in a seemingly insoluble dilemma. They express it this way: "It is easy for me to honor Jesus—he was always loving and lived a perfect life. My husband is not perfect. As a matter of fact, he has many obvious weaknesses and has done and said some things that make it difficult for me to respect him." This is a legitimate concern and a realistic problem with which wives must wrestle. So what is the solution?

First, you must once again remember the way God has ordered the marriage relationship. The husband is the head of the wife. You must respect your husband *because of the role of marital leadership* God has given him, not because of what he has or has not done. When you honor your husband, you honor God, who designed marriage and designated the husband the leader. If you rebel against God's plan here, you will rebel against it in other ways. You show you are more confident in the world's way or in your way than in God's way.

Second, you must realize that respect is given, not just earned. Wives can *choose* to honor their husbands in spite of their imperfections. It is true that Jesus won admiration by living a perfect life, so certainly husbands need to merit respect by being men of character and integrity. But no matter how good a man may be, he has faults, and no one will know them better than you will as his wife! You must then decide to give respect anyway, and to focus on your husband's good qualities instead of his flaws.

Respect Means Submission

> Wives, submit to your husbands as to the Lord. For the husband is the head of the wife as Christ is the head of the church, his body, of which he is the Savior. Now as the church submits to Christ, so also wives should submit to their husbands in everything (Ephesians 5:22-24).

The Bible clearly teaches that God places the husband in the role of leader in the marriage relationship. His role is compared to Christ's headship over the church, a position that obviously involves leadership. And while God gives firm directives that the husband exercise his headship in a Christlike fashion of love, sacrifice and sensitivity, there is not in any of these instructions a reduction in his God-given position as leader.

The attitude of respect for a husband that the Scriptures urge upon the wife must be followed up with the action of submission to his leadership. To do anything less is either to rebel directly against what God has said or is to merely give it lip-service. Submission is the practical outworking of respect in real life.

The word for "submission" in the original language is a very strong one. It has in its meaning "to line up under" and was sometimes used in a military context. At its heart is the concept of giving up your rights and subordinating or subjecting yourself to another.

What Submission Is Not

Before we go any further, we need to explain what is *not* involved in a woman submitting to her husband. Some women shy away from this concept because they think of it as being something weak and demeaning. Other women believe that showing respect to their husbands means compromising their principles to please him. Neither of these extremes is what the Bible teaches, nor are they what we want to encourage in this book.

Submission is not...	Submission is...
• being untruthful	• speaking the truth lovingly, wisely and with proper timing
• violating God's word or the laws of the land	• encouraging your husband to do the righteous thing and adapting in matters of opinion
• violating your conscience	• being content when everything does not go your way
• shifting responsibility for your decisions onto your husband, or letting your husband make all the decisions alone	• assuming full responsibility for your decisions and working together with your husband to make the best decision
• a sign of a lack of intelligence and weak convictions	• the hallmark of a wise and strong woman
• a trait of a woman with a weak temperament and personality	• an attribute of a strong woman who understands her role in her husband's life

Submission in the Bible is an honorable and noble attitude. Jesus gave up his rights and submitted himself to God (Philippians 2:6-11). It is the church's glory to submit herself to Christ (Ephesians 5:24). Church members are to lovingly and respectfully submit to church leaders (1 Thessalonians

5:12; Hebrews 13:17) and citizens are to submit to their governments (1 Peter 2:13-17).

Submission is, at its heart, a practical issue. There are many relationships in life that simply cannot function without it. Consider these examples: parents and children, employers and employees, teachers and students, coaches and athletes—just to name a few. Without the willing submission of someone in each of these situations, there can be no effectual relationship or accomplishment. How many times have we seen chaos in the home, classroom, workplace or athletic arena because of lack of submission?

Unwise leadership and abuse of power will happen in an imperfect world, but they do not negate the need for leaders to lead or followers to follow! What we need are better leaders and followers, not an abandonment of the concept. Certainly there is a time to stand up for what is right and to not allow ourselves (or others) to be taken advantage of—but this is not the same as the habitual attitude of rejecting God-given authority and continually chafing against leadership.

A wife who struggles with the concept of the leadership of her husband is in actuality fighting against God. A wife who accepts the idea in theory but who is always nagging, arguing with or subtly resisting her husband is doing the same. Such women either disdain their husbands as weaklings or compete with them as rivals. In my observation, women who do not respect and submit to their husbands end up destroying their own happiness—they do not find peace within themselves or with their husbands. Such situations are displeasing to God and end up leaving wives (and husbands!) frustrated, insecure and angry.

How different are the marriages in which wives understand and embrace this concept! Such women do not seek to dominate their mates, but discover a role that enhances their own talents and those of their husbands as well. They find their confidence not from having to be in charge, but from their relationships with God. They understand that God, in his wisdom, has given them a position that ultimately results in freedom and in a wonderful experience of married love.

As I said earlier, we do not live in a perfect world. What if you find yourself in a situation in which your husband is abusing you or one in which he will not lead? How can you demonstrate an attitude of respect and submission? Let me give you a few pointers, and urge you if you are in this situation to immediately obtain the wisest and most godly counsel you can find.

If you are in a situation of abuse:

- Do not compromise your commitment to God, his church, the law, or your conscience.

- Do your best to deal forthrightly and firmly with your husband yourself.

- If you are in a position of physical danger, get out of it.

- If you are in a position in which you are being destroyed as a person, either work for change or remove yourself from the situation. (Be especially careful here to seek wise counsel. Separation should be a last resort, and hopefully only temporary.)

- Retain a respectful attitude toward your husband even when you must confront him with his wrongdoing. (A great example of how to deal with a strongly opinionated man who is set on the wrong course is found in Abigail's interaction with David in 1 Samuel 25. Though she was not yet his wife, she showed wisdom, firmness and humility in a very trying situation.)

If your husband will not lead or leads weakly:

- Let him know you need and desire him to be more assertive and decisive.

- Seek his opinion and input before making decisions— do not rush ahead if he delays in making a decision.

- Listen carefully to what he says—he may be making more of an effort to lead than you realize.

- When he does make a decision, support him even if it turns out not to have been the perfect choice.

- Set aside time to be alone with him so that he will be comfortable (and refreshed!) to have more involved conversations with you. (This is especially needful if you are quick to make decisions and your husband is more reflective.)

- Above all, do not allow yourself to develop a nagging, pushy or contentious nature.

Wives, are you still reading? Or have you given up on this book as a hopelessly outdated return to Neanderthal thinking? Put those scissors away! If you cut out these pages you will be missing out on the very ingredient that could turn your marriage around. Read this section and the Scriptures referenced over and over, and see if it doesn't start making sense! Now let's move forward and learn more about how to show respect in practice.

Respect Him

Believe in him. Believe the best of your husband! Believe that he can do great things. See the talent in him that others may not see. Believe that he can achieve more in the future than he has in the past. He may never become as great as you think he can be, but he very likely will never rise above your contempt. He must know and feel that you believe better things of him than anyone else does. How many men would accomplish more with their lives if their wives believed they could?

Focus on his good qualities. You picked this guy out of all the other men on earth because you saw some pretty outstanding qualities in him. Don't ever forget what those good qualities are! Sadly, after we get married, we may begin to focus on our spouses' weaknesses more than on their strengths.

We can even become critical of their strengths since they are usually different from our own. Get rid of this negative mindset! Instead, focus on the good. Be continually thankful for his good traits in your heart and with your words. You will not make him a better man by harping on his weaknesses or habitually thinking about all of his faults.

Praise him. Put your appreciation into words. Tell him on a daily basis how great you think he is, how much he means to you and how much good you see in him. When he does something right, say so. Thank him for doing the everyday things that you can often take for granted—things like working hard on the job, being reliable, being a good father, being thoughtful, etc. Men sometimes appear not to need encouragement and praise, but they do. They usually don't get much appreciation in their jobs or from other men! Your praise can be an oasis of refreshment in a man's difficult world.

Seek to adapt and to please. Adapt yourself to the man you married. Don't try to shape him into your mold or into your image. Do the little things he likes that will make his life easier and more pleasant. Learn to make his favorite dinner and to dress (within reason!) the way he prefers. Build a household that is comfortable for him in terms of atmosphere and decor. Remember, he is the head of the household in the same way Jesus is the head of the church, and just as the goal of the church is to please Jesus, so a wife's aim is to please her husband. Make that your goal no matter how many magazine articles or talk shows say it is foolish. The family should revolve more around your husband than your children or yourself. Your husband will have plenty of adapting and changing to do, but do your part to adapt to him first. (And in case you are wondering, I had plenty of encouragement from my wife to write this!)

Help others to respect him. Carry your attitude of respect for him out into your world. If you have children, frequently express to them how much you admire their father. Compliment him in front of your relatives. When you are with your husband's friends and business associates, show respect in the way you treat and address him. Convey the same attitude in the manner you speak about him when he is absent. If a man's wife tears him down, who is left to build him up?

Complement Him

People usually marry someone who has strengths they do not, and their spouses marry them for the same reason. As a wife, your strengths are a complement to your husband's weaknesses. This may be your greatest value to his success in life. You will make him a man he could never be without you, and the two of you are greater together than you would be as individuals.

Make an effort to balance your husband's character weaknesses. If he is dynamic and powerful but tends to be harsh and overly aggressive, your gentleness can make him a kinder man. If he is a perfectionist and is so critical of himself (and others) that he rarely finishes a project and finds it difficult to work with people, then help him to be more positive, faithful and accepting. If he is unmotivated and indecisive, encourage him to get up and get going. If he is a warm and outgoing, but tends to lack discipline, then assist him in getting organized, staying on a schedule and showing attention to details. Learn how to accomplish this in a positive manner and not by nagging. Realize the importance of your role in this area. It could make the difference between your husband's ultimate success and failure in life.

I am a person with strong convictions, intense drive and a compelling desire to do things excellently. My weaknesses are that I tend to lose sight of larger issues, become negative and get buried in detail. My wife, on the other hand, sees the big picture and does not worry so much about the specifics of how things will get done. She sees the ultimate goal and is excellent at figuring out the direction in which we need to go. I have learned to ask her advice, solicit her opinion and listen when she speaks. She has helped me tremendously, and because I seek her advice, she has developed greater confidence. I respect her deeply for her talents—talents that I do not naturally possess. I respect her even more highly now than I did when we were first married because her abilities have continued to emerge the longer we have been together.

Wives, begin using your talents to help your husbands. Don't hold back! Don't wait until you are upset or critical before you offer to pitch in and help. Do so with the attitude of : "*I love my husband more than anyone else does. I don't want him to fail; I want him to succeed. If, by getting in there, giving advice and helping him out, I can make a difference in his success, then I am going to do it for his sake.*"

Love Him

It is my observation that a woman's love, demeanor and spirit sets the tone for an entire household. Wife, if you love your husband deeply and affectionately, it will make your home a wonderful place. If your demeanor is sunny, cheerful and encouraging, it will make your husband a happy man, and your children contented and joyful.

Your husband should know you love him more than anyone else on earth—more than you love your father, your mother or your children. He must know that you are more devoted to meeting his needs and being close to him than to anyone else in your life, except God himself.

A man needs the tender grace of a woman's love. It softens his heart and makes him gentler, kinder and more compassionate. Your love will help to create a better father, a more devoted friend and a man of deeper sensitivity. Without a woman's love, a man can become sour, harsh and bitter. Men often function daily in a highly competitive environment in which self-interest rules and hardheaded aggressiveness is rewarded. A woman's love can make the difference in a man becoming a force for good in such a harsh environment rather than being swallowed up by it. Certainly, some wives are in similar environments, and both should seek to build each other up.

<hr>

The longer I live with my wife the more I respect her great qualities of kindness, love and sensitivity. The way she handles the pressures of life, the weaknesses of the people around her and the faults and immaturity of our children has challenged me to be a better man. Her example of forgiveness in the face of maltreatment by others has enabled me to soften my heart when I felt injustices were done to me. Her greatness of vision and refusal to be pulled into petty disputes and quarrels has enabled me to lift myself above bitterness and resentment. Her love for me in spite of my weaknesses, even after seeing me at my worst, has taught me what it means to be loved unconditionally. Her belief in the best in me has inspired me to strive for greater heights, and though I may never become the person my wife believes I can be, I am a far better man for trying.

It is my prayer that each of you wives who reads these words will find in them the inspiration and encouragement to respect, complement and love your husband. You are the most important person in his life, and for the most part, he lives or dies, stands or falls, and succeeds or fails based upon his relationship with you.

One More Thought...

Speaking from a woman's perspective, I will add several observations regarding the role of wives in marriage. Although I will specifically address the woman's role, some of the thoughts will apply to husbands as well.

Years ago, when I first turned to the Bible for wisdom and guidance for my life, I would constantly read the scriptures that discussed marriage, especially the ones addressed to wives. At that time I used *The New Testament in Modern English* by J.B. Phillips. His translation of a certain word to describe the wife's role in marriage greatly influenced my life. Ephesians 5:22 states, "You wives must learn to *adapt* yourselves to your husband as you submit yourselves to the Lord." Likewise, Colossians 3:18 said, "Wives *adapt* yourselves to your husbands, that your marriage may be a Christian unity" (emphasis mine).

Unfortunately, many of us still have a strong aversion to the word "submit," the word most often (and accurately!) used in our Bible translations. For some of you, the word has negative connotations. As wives we certainly do need to submit, but sometimes it is difficult to understand exactly what that word means. The word *adapt* is only a partial definition of *submit*, but it is one I could more easily grasp and practically apply. To adapt to my husband meant I needed to accept and build my life around the man I married—not around how I *wished* he would be, but around how he actually *was*!

How many of our marriages are disintegrating every day because we are not happy with certain things about our spouses? Instead of accepting their weaknesses along with their strengths, we become resentful or discontent. For many of us, the walk down the aisle marks the beginning of a lifelong commitment to change our mate into who we want him or her to be instead of the beginning of a life in which two very imperfect people put their strengths together to become one closer-to-perfect couple.

Practically, what does it mean for me to learn to adapt to the man I married? It means that I accept and appreciate him for who he is. Is he moody at times? That is the kind of man I married, and I will adapt to that. Not only will I accept his moodiness, but I will even learn to appreciate all of the strengths of sensitivity and passion for life that accompany such a personality. If he is a talker, then I will become a great listener. Is he quiet? I will learn to "hear" the things he feels even when few words are spoken. Is he intense and serious? I will admire that and become a person of stronger convictions myself. Does he love to play sports? Even if I do not naturally share his enthusiasm for sports, I will be glad he is athletic and learn to enjoy his sporting interests.

You may have married an ambitious person, or one who is more complacent (or even lazy!); a person with a temper, or one who is laid back; a person who is strong, or one who is weak; a person who is fanatical about order and cleanliness, or someone who is disorganized and terribly messy. Are all of these qualities admirable and fun to live with? No! But this is the person you married, and in order for your marriage to grow, you must adapt to him or her. You must learn to appreciate all there is to respect and accept all those things that are difficult. Acceptance does not mean that you say nothing about things that are wrong or things that hurt you, or even those that just bother you. Say something—but say it as you would like it to be said to you, and realize that you still belong to each other, flaws and all. Great marriages are built when we concentrate more on the things that we admire and respect in each other than on all the things we are determined to change in each other.

When we as wives learn to adapt to our husbands, great things happen. As we submit and adapt, they become more confident and feel closer to us. We learn to trust in God, and come to understand what it means to accept someone for who he is, and to extend God's grace to him as it has been extended to us. And we end up becoming more unified and more in love, and becoming better people together than we ever would have been apart.

Geri Laing

PART 2

·Romance·

CHAPTER 5

The Plan

God saw all that he had made,
and it was very good. And there was
evening, and there was morning—
the sixth day.

GENESIS 1:31

Imagine yourself sitting in a darkened room filled with people. Music plays, softly at first, then with a rising volume and quickening tempo. The crowd strains forward, looking at a dimly lit stage. As the lights slowly brighten, the audience, becoming raucous with expectation, stares transfixed at a draped table. In teasing concert with the intensifying chords, the drape is slowly pulled back, revealing...a tossed salad! The crowd goes wild. "Pour on the Blue Cheese!" bellows the big guy sitting next to you. "Yeah, and how about a little *fresh ground pepper!*" yells a businessman across the room. "What in the world is going on here?" you ask yourself in shocked amazement. But there is more! In rhythm with pounding percussion the drape is pulled farther back, exposing...peas and carrots! People stand on their chairs, whistling and hooting. From a group of women seated near the stage, one runs up and slips a dollar bill under the table cloth, giggling with delight as her girlfriends cheer her on, "Go Susie, Go Susie, Go Susie!"

Dozens of onlookers abandon their seats and flock closer to the front. The music escalates to a deafening crescendo. The tablecloth is drawn back farther, baring the main course...tuna casserole! People scream, rant and rave. Security guards form a cordon around the stage. They wrestle down a guy who has somehow broken through to sprint toward the table. *"Take it off! Take it all off!"* chants the crowd. With a flourish, the drape is whipped away completely. Hot apple pie a la mode! The gasping, delirious crowd is calmed only by the intervention of the descending curtain and dimming stage lights. As the house lights rise, they return to their seats, gather their belongings and file out of the room.

You are left sitting alone, trying to make sense of what you have witnessed. You come up with two conclusions: *These people are starving to death, and they have some very weird ideas about food.*

———

Perhaps our striptease story can help us see just how foolish, confused and twisted we are about sex. Our situation is desperate and it is deteriorating. From the talk shows to the classroom, sexuality is debated and discussed. Everyone has an opinion, and the search for sexual fulfillment is becoming more outlandish and frightening. Pornography, masturbation, premarital sex, cohabitation and adultery—these deviances are old news. Cybersex, homosexuality, lesbianism, bisexuality, gay marriage, transvestitism, sadomasochism and pedophilia—these are on the cutting edge today! Tell me, what sexual deviance *isn't* openly talked about and even promoted by somebody?

It seems everyone is hungry for sex, yet few are satisfied. Sexuality is flaunted in public, yet often not enjoyed in private. In spite of our obsessive, outrageous preoccupation with sex, we have not attained the satisfaction, fulfillment and excitement we crave. The more desperately we try, the greater our despair. Sooner or later we need to wake up and realize that there are no answers in the places we have been searching. We must look somewhere else.

In the midst of our failure there is a simple, profound truth that gives hope: *God has a plan.* It is not just a good plan. It is the best plan, and it works without fail. We can understand it, and we can follow it. We can check out of the strip-tease scene and get into the real action!

God's Plan Is Good

God did not make sex dirty, shameful or evil—it is we who have done that. We have dragged it from its pristine glory and have stained it with selfishness and perversion. It is we who have turned its great power for good to unspeakable horrors of destruction, degradation and misery. It is we who have turned the sex act into a curse word.

Think about it. The slang term for sexual union has become an expression of insult!

It is we who have a problem with sex, not God. God created sex and he did a good job of it. After he made everything, he looked it all over and said, "It is good" (Genesis 1:31). Because of this, Adam and Eve could gaze upon each other's naked bodies without sin, shame or self-consciousness (Genesis 2:25). Sex was not the "forbidden fruit" of the Garden of Eden; that was real fruit from a real tree (Genesis 3:1-17). Sex was not prohibited to Adam and Eve; it was expected of them! Adam was to be "united to his wife" and they were to "become one flesh" (Genesis 2:24). Besides, God had already told Adam and Eve to have children, to "be fruitful and increase in number" (Genesis 1:28). Given the technology of the day they had but one method to carry this out—and I trust our readers know what it was!

There is a strain of religious thinking that holds to the belief that to be spiritually pure and sincerely devoted to God, we ought to avoid sex altogether. Behind this notion lies the misguided thinking that sex is inherently evil, and God's true servants cannot be tainted with it. It results in the exaltation of virginity (e.g., in the doctrine of The Perpetual Virginity of Mary) and the requirement that spiritual leaders give up marriage and take vows of celibacy. How different is the clear teaching of the Bible, which honors marriage and requires bishops (also called overseers or elders) to be married men. (See 1 Timothy 3:1-7, 4:1-5; Titus 1: 5-9; Hebrews 13:4.)

Unfortunately, some churches and religions speak of sex and sexuality only in terms of its abuse. They present sex primarily as a dangerous temptation, as a menace to our souls. This emphasis can result in an unhealthy view of sex that can harm our marriages and render us more susceptible to temptation. While God does define and condemn sexual sin, he does not view sex negatively. The Scriptures teach us to "hate what is evil" (Romans 12:9) but also to "overcome evil with good" (Romans 12:21). This is the balance we need. We must see the terrible danger of promiscuity, and with equal fervor claim sex as a joyful privilege of married life. *Sin is the enemy, not sex!*

We must get into our heads once and for all that sex is good. It is a gift of God, intended for our happiness. It enables husbands and wives to express their love, draw close, give and receive pleasure, and conceive children. It is beautiful, wonderful, satisfying, needful, natural and noble. And all of that is good!

How the Plan Works

God's plan is for sexual intimacy to be experienced only in marriage. Marriage is defined in the Bible as a relationship between a man and a woman committed in love to each other for as long as they both live (Matthew 19:4-6). Within that framework, sex can and should be regularly enjoyed. Outside of that relationship, it is strictly forbidden and is always wrong.

Sex is wrong before marriage and outside of marriage. Sexual lust is wrong. Sexual activity with any person other than our marriage partner is wrong. Sexual activity with someone of the same sex (homosexuality) is sinful under any circumstance. No one is created or born to be a homosexual. It is learned, sinful behavior. God has spoken clearly to these issues, and it is not a matter of debate with him. It has nothing to do with culture, politics or genetics; it has everything to do with God's eternal, revealed will. (See Exodus 20:14; Mark 7:20-23; Romans 1:24-27; 1 Corinthians 6:9-20; Hebrews 13:4.) A person's background may contribute to his or her being more easily tempted by a particular sin—e.g. promiscuity, pornography, prostitution or homosexuality—but sin is still sin and can be overcome by those who have the desire to please God. No one is genetically predisposed to live a life-style that is contrary to God's plan.

God's Plan: Best and Better

The best sex is married sex. The most exciting, fulfilling and thrilling sex takes place in the marriage bed, not the bed of illicit sex. Why? Because God has designed sex to thrive in a permanent commitment, not a temporary arrangement, and the only relationship that is secure is the marriage relationship. It is a lie that the greatest, most intense sexual pleasure is found in situations that are temporary or forbidden—the adulterous affair, the prostitute, the one-night stand or the premarital liaison. This is a myth promoted by movies, television and cheap romance novels, and we had better not swallow it. If God is good (which he is) and God wants us to have a great marriage (which he does), then his plan for sex is better than the world's plan.

Married sex gets better as the years go by. It becomes increasingly intimate, pleasurable and satisfying. Why? Once again, the answer lies in the permanence of the relationship. Love and passion flourish in the soil of lifetime dedication. As we know each other longer and better, we become more comfortable in our lovemaking. Modesty and insecurity give way to confidence and familiarity. Both husband and wife feel more free to let go, be themselves and enjoy themselves. There is no pressure to prove ourselves or to perform—we have a relationship that goes beyond those worldly games. So what if there is a night that doesn't go well or that is less than memorable—we'll be back! We will just love each other more, and together we will overcome the challenges.

I have often said facetiously that honeymoons are wasted on amateurs. It's just that those married longer have had more time to master the art of pleasing their spouses. From years of counseling, I have learned that couples who grow in their love, stay close to each other, grow spiritually and communicate freely have a love life that is increasingly exciting and satisfying with the passing of years. They not only still have the fire—it burns brighter and hotter!

The Rose

We can understand how marriage works by comparing it to a rosebush. Commitment to God and to one another are the life-giving roots of the plant. The proper fulfilling of our role as a husband or a wife is the supporting stalk. Communication is the energy-producing leaves. The thorns have their purpose to warn any adulterous interloper to get away and stay away forever! And romantic love? It is the flower! Sexual love is the fragrance, the beauty and the crowning glory of the plant. It is not the life, as some mistakenly believe, but it *is* the joy!

When every part of the plant functions properly, the flower flourishes, but if there is weakness anywhere, the flower is the first to suffer. Its withering is the symptom of deeper maladies.

If your love life is not living up to the plan that God has designed, then something in your marriage is wrong that must be fixed, and *can* be fixed. In the next chapter we will identify these problems so that our marriages may be rid of them and blossom with the beauty, fragrance and glory of romantic love.

CHAPTER 6

The Problems

Catch for us the foxes,
    the little foxes
that ruin the vineyards,
    our vineyards that are in bloom.

SONG OF SONGS 2:15

The Symptoms Noticed

The sexual aspect of many marriages is far from what God wants it to be. His promises are great, but the claimants are few. We allow a variety of "little foxes," and some not so little ones, to get into our vineyard and spoil the good things God designed for us to enjoy. Some experience *function without fulfillment*: dutifully going through the motions of lovemaking without the bonding and unity of hearts. Others experience *fizzle, not sizzle*: no excitement, no anticipation, no creativity and no thrill. Many grapple with the problem of *fighting, not fun*: arguing, bickering, harsh words and hard feelings destroying the tender intimacies of romantic love. And many others face the problem of *fading frequency*: They are distracted, disinterested, bored or simply out of the habit of experiencing this most special of moments.

Failure to recognize these problems is extremely dangerous. If you accept any of them as the norm, you are inviting disaster. You are standing on a trap door that can at any moment fly open, leaving you or your spouse to fall into bitterness, lust, adultery and divorce. To adequately deal with these problems, we must go beyond the symptoms and discover and eradicate their underlying causes. In this chapter we will look at some of these underlying causes—problems that undermine our intimacy and create distance in our relationships.

The Problems Described

Pattern of Neglect

In many marriages the problem is simple and uncomplicated: We are neglecting our romantic relationship. With the busyness of life and a few challenges here and there, we find ourselves less and less sexually involved with our spouses. In too many cases the partner with the lesser desire sets the tone. But listen to what the Scriptures clearly teach:

> The husband should fulfill his marital duty to his wife, and likewise the wife to her husband. The wife's body does not belong to her alone but also to her husband. In the same way, the husband's body does not belong to him alone but also to his wife. Do not deprive each other except by mutual consent and for a time, so that you may devote yourselves to prayer. Then come together again so that Satan will not tempt you because of your lack of self-control (1 Corinthians 7:3-5).

This passage teaches us several vital principles about sex in marriage. First, satisfying our partners is a responsibility given by God to both husband and wife. When the scripture above speaks of fulfilling our "marital duty" (v. 3), it is most assuredly not referring to paying the bills, taking out the garbage or doing the dishes! The happy duty here enjoined is that of making love to our spouses and satisfying their sexual needs.

Second, we learn that our bodies are not solely our own, but are jointly possessed by our mates. We should not withhold ourselves from our spouses except by mutual agreement and then only "for a time" (v. 5). It is this last principle that addresses the subject of frequency of lovemaking in marriage.

How much sex is enough? The answer is really quite simple: *You are having enough sex when both people are completely satisfied. If either partner is not content, then increase your frequency until both the husband's and wife's needs are met.*

Right about now, some of you women are saying, "I had

better hide this book before my husband sees it. If he ever reads this chapter, I'm done for. I will have no time for a social life, my job, or to eat and sleep. Life as I know it will be *over*." (And there are some men saying the same thing about their wives as well!) To you of anxious heart I say, Fear not. This won't be as exhausting as you think!

Instead of selfishly worrying and resisting, be warm, available and responsive. When your partner gets accustomed to the amazing concept that you are accessible and positive about lovemaking, his or her initial euphoria and aggressiveness will in all likelihood abate and you will settle into a pattern that you can live with very comfortably. (Practically speaking, I would recommend that you reduce the length of some of your romantic times; shorter encounters have their place!)

If husbands and wives practice the law of love and are more eager to please than to be pleased, the issue of frequency can be solved. Remember that you are no longer two, but one—your body belongs to your mate and not to you alone. Learn to think unselfishly and to see your marriage as a partnership. The spouse with the greater desire will recognize that there are times when self-denial is the loving thing. Likewise, the more easily satisfied partner will grasp that giving themselves cheerfully, even when they feel no personal need, is the way to joy and peace in the marriage. It is better for one of you to have more than enough sex than for the other to have less than enough!

Most couples will find that anywhere from one encounter a day to one per week will be sufficient. But I must add that this varies depending upon a myriad of factors, so we should avoid setting up a numeric goal. Most couples find that with the passing of time, their love life goes through change and adjustment, and their needs and desires will alter accordingly.

Pain from the Past

"'Forget the former things; do not dwell on the past. See, I am doing a new thing! Now it springs up; do you not perceive it? I am making a way in the desert and streams in the wasteland'" (Isaiah 43:18-19).

Because sex is wrapped up tightly with emotion, and is deeply connected to our inner being, past sexual experiences can have profound and long-lasting effects. Distant events of which we may have no conscious recollection can powerfully shape sexual behavior in our marriages today.

What are these experiences, and how do they affect us?

Sexual Abuse. Incidents of sexual abuse from your childhood or later life can hurt your present. If you were fondled, molested, attacked or raped, it has affected you, and may be affecting you still. Events such as these, even if buried deep in your memory, can severely impair your ability to give and receive sexual love in your marriage.

Do not allow your life to be ruined by sexual abuse. Get help from qualified Christian advisors. Get the facts and your feelings out in the open. Come to understand what happened and how it has affected and is affecting you. If possible, reconcile directly with the other person. Forgive them, even if they do not respond as they should. Take any rightful personal responsibility. Accept the fact that this has occurred; do not spend the rest of your life vainly wishing otherwise. Get rid of any residual attitudes of bitterness or resentment. Do not blame God for your pain. Instead, let him heal you emotionally. Remember that God can bring good out of the worst experiences, and trust him to work out his great plan for your life.

Abortion. The Bible teaches that God is sovereign over human life (Exodus 20:13) and that our bodies do not belong to us, but to God (1 Corinthians 6:19-20). While there are some situations that pose difficult ethical questions, the vast majority of abortions are performed for purely selfish personal reasons, and are sinful and offensive to God.

Any sin we commit affects our whole life; the influence of abortion is especially powerful. Even in cases where a woman is intellectually convinced that it is morally acceptable, abortion can diminish her ability to love, to feel good about herself and to enjoy sex. Abortion can destroy a woman's innocence, damage her capacity to be close, and cause her to harden her heart. Its legacy is guilt and pain.

If you have had an abortion, you must come to grips with what you have done. You must ask God for forgiveness and for a clear conscience that only his grace can bring. You will probably need help from mature Christian advisors to see you through this process.

Premarital sexual activity. If you were sexually promiscuous before marriage, it may affect your ability to enjoy sex now. You may have developed a lustful, selfish attitude that taints the loving, innocent joy of marital sex. Disturbing memories of encounters with past sexual partners can invade your minds even as you make love to your husband or wife. How can you relax and have a great time when you have so many vivid memories of past sins? God's plan is for us to face our past honestly, repent openly, accept forgiveness humbly and focus on the joys of married love gratefully.

If you and your spouse had sex with each other before marriage, there will be negative consequences. There may be a lack of respect for your mate and for yourself. There could be feelings of dirtiness, shame or brooding anger that come from feeling that your innocence was stolen. Again, openness and forgiveness of each other is imperative, and you may need help to see this one through.

Sexually transmitted diseases. In our day and age sexually transmitted diseases (STDs) are at epidemic proportions. Those who become disciples of Jesus in time to commit to God's plan for sex will be blessed and spared from this problem. However, many who commit their lives to Christ were sexually active before and, as a result, did become infected with some disease. As is well known, some of these afflictions, like AIDS, are fatal. Other diseases like genital herpes are not fatal, but are incurable, and will present ongoing challenges. (Certainly, those contemplating marriage should get sound advice and be very open with a prospective spouse about any such situations.) It is not unusual to find situations where two people were sexually active, caught an STD, got married and then later became Christians. In such circumstances we have found that they are sometimes too ashamed to talk about how outbreaks of the disease interfere with sexual relations and are painful reminders of past sins.

These knotty problems are usually far beyond our ability to work out ourselves; we need outside help, and we must not let embarrassment stop us from seeking it. We must do whatever is best for our marriages.

With any of these issues be sure the help you get comes from proven Christian leaders. Get everything out in the open, take responsibility for your sin, reconcile your relationship and experience the refreshment that repentance and forgiveness can bring.

There is far more that can be said about dealing with the past than we can adequately address given the scope of this book, but perhaps we have made a small beginning. With God's healing love at work in your marriage, you have every reason to hope that you will experience freedom and release from the pain of your past.

Pregnancy

Lovemaking can certainly lead to pregnancy, and pregnancy can lead to a diminished sex life! With couples who have lost their frequency and joy in sexual intercourse, one common thread is that the problems began when the wife became pregnant. I have heard it said like this: "Things were great when we were newlyweds. But after the pregnancy we began to have less time together, and we just never really got our sex life back again after the baby was born."

This is sad, wrong and dangerous. Too many men fall into lust, masturbation, pornography and adultery during the months of pregnancy. At a time when our wives need us the most, we can become selfish and unfaithful. Wives can allow the physical and emotional trials of pregnancy to keep them from sexual intimacy. They can become physically and emotionally distant from their husbands while they are carrying their unborn children. Let me say with all the conviction I have: *Pregnancy and childbirth will bring challenges into the bedroom, but these challenges must be overcome at all cost.*

Commit to each other to enjoy a warm, exciting love life right up to the birth of the baby. Only under doctor's orders should there be an elimination or reduction of your sexual activity during pregnancy. Even when having intercourse is not wise, there are a variety of ways to give to one another sexually and maintain physical and emotional intimacy. After childbirth, resume relations as soon as the wife is physically able. (This should be a matter of several weeks, not months.) Children should be conceived, gestated, born and raised in an atmosphere of love between their mom and dad. We do our marriages and our children grave harm when we take the joy of sexual love out of our relationship at this critical time.

Progeny

The rigors of raising children can exact a heavy toll on your love life. Mothers can become fatigued, frumpy and fretful. Fathers can get frazzled and frustrated. While these pressures are to be expected, they cannot justify the demise of your sex life.

My wife tells me, and other women confirm, that for a new mother, holding and cuddling an infant supplies a sort of fulfillment and satisfaction that can diminish a woman's appetite for sex. I have never met a man who relates to or comprehends this phenomenon! Your husband's sexual desires are in no way reduced by caring for a newborn. His need for you is the same. New mothers, you simply must not allow your diminished need to keep you away from your husband. Don't be selfish! Give yourself to him physically even though your desires are weaker than before. The time will come when your sexual appetite will resurge, but if you have neglected your husband, you will find your marriage in disarray, and the children you thought you were loving so unselfishly will pay the price for your folly.

A couple needs privacy. Your bedroom must be a place of sanctuary and security. Don't let it become a nursery. Newborns may be kept in their parents' bedroom for a short while without harming the marriage, but they must have a separate room as soon as possible. What is best is to give babies their own rooms with their own little beds, and teach them to sleep there! Allowing older kids to sleep with parents is likewise harmful to a happy sexual life. If children become afraid or have a bad dream, go into their room, comfort them, and let them go back to sleep. If they are ill and need you by their side through the night, then lie down in their room. Permitting children into your bed is indulgent and overprotective.

You will spoil your kids, ruin your romantic life, and your entire family will ultimately suffer for it.

Lock your bedroom door when you need privacy. You cannot relax and enjoy a romantic night in bed if you are fearful of interruption. How many times, as the passion was heating up, has one of you inquired, "Are you *sure* the door is locked?" Nothing can bring us closer to cardiac arrest than the ill-timed entry of a child into the bedroom—and some of us have the fingernail marks on the ceiling above our beds to prove it!

Is this being selfish? Does this mean you are a neglectful mom or a heartless dad? Absolutely not! What you are saying to your children (and to one another) is that your marriage is sacred and worth protecting. The kids will be better off and more secure for it. They will learn to respect your privacy and not be selfish and demanding. You and your spouse will enjoy a continuing love life, and a sanctuary of peace and quiet within a busy home.

Purity Lost

> Marriage should be honored by all, and the marriage bed kept pure, for God will judge the adulterer and all the sexually immoral (Hebrews 13:4).

Adultery is the most devastating of marital sins. It is the only reason God allows divorce (Matthew 19:9). If you commit adultery, the consequent guilt, shame and heartache are some of the most destructive emotions you can experience. If your spouse has been unfaithful, you suffer a type of living death because the one you love is lost to you not by fate, but by his or her own choice. Adultery tears the heart as no other grief.

We cannot experience sexual fulfillment with our spouses if either of us is unfaithful. Even if we have concealed our sin, it cannot remain forever hidden. It inevitably shows itself in its corrosive effect upon our intimacy. When adultery does become known, radical steps of repentance will have to be taken to restore the marriage and the sexual relationship.

Sexual involvement on any level with someone other that
your spouse is sinful. Sexual intercourse, sexual touching,
hugging or kissing—all of this is forbidden. Flirting (engag-
ing in suggestive conversation or giving off sexual cues) is
wrong. We cannot claim innocence if we allow ourselves to
become familiar with someone else, even if it is in a joking
manner. This solemn warning against adultery, though here
issued to men, is true for both sexes:

> For the lips of an adulteress drip honey,
>   and her speech is smoother than oil;
> but in the end she is bitter as gall,
>   sharp as a double-edged sword...
> Now then, my sons, listen to me;
>   do not turn aside from what I say.
> Keep to a path far from her,
>   do not go near the door of her house
> (Proverbs 5:3-4, 7-8).

Adultery is committed first in our hearts. Before we become physically involved, we get mentally, emotionally and
visually involved:

> "You have heard that it was said, 'Do not commit adul-
> tery.' But I tell you that anyone who looks at a woman
> lustfully has already committed adultery with her in his
> heart" (Matthew 5:27-28).

For men, the pathway to adultery most easily begins with
what we see. A man who indulges himself in gazing sexually
at other women is already in sin. We must therefore learn to
discipline our eyes: "Let your eyes look straight ahead, fix
your gaze directly before you" (Proverbs 4:25). Whether it is
on the street, in the office or in the classroom; whether it is in
viewing movies or television or looking at magazines; whether
it is fantasizing about real or invented illicit sexual encounters, lust is absolutely wrong and must be resisted and overcome at any cost.

> If your right eye causes you to sin, gouge it out and throw it
> away. It is better for you to lose one part of your body than

> for your whole body to be thrown into hell. And if your
> right hand causes you to sin, cut it off and throw it away. It
> is better for you to lose one part of your body than for your
> whole body to go into hell (Matthew 5:29-30).

Some men, at the first hint of temptation, are quickly over-whelmed with guilt and an accusing conscience. We do not help our own cause in the battle against lust when we overreact in this manner. There is no sin in noticing that a woman is pretty—it is to be expected that men notice feminine beauty. Admiration of this sort should not necessarily be regarded as temptation, although it can lead to it. Temptation occurs when we are drawn to look with the wrong motive. Sin occurs when we look in order to lust—when our look is coupled with sexual desire. We must learn to distinguish between these different mindsets (admiration, temptation and lust), so that we can avoid both the peril of lust and the trap of an oversensitive conscience.

A woman's temptations usually follow a different path. Often they begin with the emotions of friendship, and not with physical appearance. The physical proceeds from the emotional. A man is kind, friendly and considerate to you. He could be a friend, a neighbor, a coworker or someone you admire. He is attentive, sensitive and thoughtful. He makes you laugh. You then find yourself becoming drawn to him physically.

While it is fine for married women to have male friends, there must be a proper distance maintained. Your heart can deceive you. You must learn to care as a sister and to be hon-est with yourself if there is anything more to your feelings than innocent friendship. Women who do not feel close to their husbands are the most vulnerable here and need to be aware of the challenges that such feelings can bring.

Like men, women must decisively resist sexual tempta-tion. Immediate steps must be taken to remove yourself from a relationship with a man who is drawing you away from your husband. One of the first moves, for both men and women, is to confess our temptations and sins to a mature Christian of the same sex so that we can receive guidance and be held accountable for our attitudes and behavior. Don't try to handle it alone! We must be willing to take any action, however radical, to block lust from getting a foothold in our lives.

Before leaving this section, let me address the issue of solitary sexual experience (masturbation). Although the Bible does not refer to it directly, there are the strongest of reasons for saying that masturbation is a perversion of God's plan and God's way. God addresses and deals with sexual experience in a positive sense only in the context of married love. God designed and ordained sex to be enjoyed with our spouses, and that is the only place where it is permitted. Masturbation is an attempt to please ourselves. It alienates a person from his or her spouse and is the refuge of those who lack self-control and are unwilling or unable to work out a satisfactory marriage relationship. Even if someone claims to be imagining sex with his or her spouse while masturbating, the ultimate result is to deprive the spouse of attention and love. In the words of psychiatrist John White, "[Masturbation] takes what was meant to be a powerful urge encouraging a close personal relationship but aborts it. That which was meant to be shared is squandered in solitude."[1] Masturbation is a selfish, enslaving practice that opens us up to lustful fantasies and other sexual perversions. Masturbation frustrates God's plan. It does not fulfill it. We must stay away from it.

It is encouraging to know that we are not left to fight the battle for sexual purity alone. Jesus "has been tempted in every way, just as we are—yet was without sin" (Hebrews 4:15). He understands temptation, and can help us overcome it. When we are tempted and if we falter, we have the freedom to "approach the throne of grace with confidence, so that we may receive mercy and find grace to help us in our time of need" (Hebrews 4:16).

Punishment

One of the worst mistakes you can make in marriage is to withhold sex to pay back your partner for wronging you! Resolve your problems and hurt feelings quickly. "'In your anger do not sin': Do not let the sun go down while you are still angry, and do not give the devil a foothold" (Ephesians 4:26-27). Don't play games with sex. Using "I have a headache" or

"Not tonight," as part of a strategy to manipulate your spouse or get your way is wrong, dishonest and destructive.

Haranguing or badgering your spouse to have sex proceeds from a mean-spirited, unloving attitude and is but another form of punishment. Men who physically force their wives to have intercourse or who purposely hurt their wives during sex are committing a serious sin and should immediately seek help. If a husband will not come forth, the wife should take swift action to secure assistance before the situation becomes more dangerous.

People and Phones

We should love people, enjoy fellowship and practice hospitality. But as wonderful as friends are, they can be an impediment to our love life. There is a time to stay up late with folks and have long talks that bond us together in friendship, but we can't *always* have other people around. There is a time to go home and to suggest that others do the same. There is a time for our guests to retire to the guest room. And don't wait until it is so late that you can only think of how exhausted you will be when the alarm goes off the next morning!

Phones are a wonderful invention, but they can ring at the wrong times. I am sure all of us have those special friends who have the uncanny ability to call at, shall we say, awkward moments. I don't know how they do it—I have wondered if it is coincidental or some sort of demonic plot. But this I know: Unless we take proper measures, the ringing phone can ruin a wonderful night.

Before a time of lovemaking, turn off the ringer on the phone to keep from being interrupted by interminable electronic jangling. "That could be my mother," whispers the wife. "The boss said he might call," mutters the husband. One of you gets out of bed, stumbles to the phone and answers it, hoping the caller does not ask, "So, what are you two doing tonight?"

Also be certain you turn down the speaker volume on your answering machine. If not, you will hear wailing voices reverberating from the machine imploring, "*Please* come to the phone. I *know* you're home tonight, and I *really* need to talk to you." Most calls can wait for a while. I urge you: Do not allow your

sex life to be ruined by well-meaning people who have no idea
what their calls are interrupting.

Physical Differences

"Male and female he created them" says the scripture (Genesis 1:27), and the difference between men and women is
clearly evident in what motivates and satisfies them sexually.
The failure to understand, appreciate and move in harmony
with these God-given traits is one of the most prominent mistakes married couples make. If, on the other hand, we learn
to work with our differences as part of the mystery that God
has built into us, the very differences that once caused conflict become a part of the wonder that makes romantic love a
joy.

Both men and women move through a sexual experience
in the following pattern:

Phase 1	**Phase 2**	**Phase 3**	**Phase 4**
Desire	Arousal	Release	Resolution

How do men and women differ as they go through these
phases?

First, men can move through Phase 1 (Desire) to Phase 2
(Arousal) very rapidly, and need far less emotional stimulation than women to do so. As a matter of fact, a man needs no
emotional reinforcement at all to become aroused. The mere
sight of his wife's body can quickly move him to Phase 2.
Women, on the other hand, need a stronger emotional con-
nection with their husbands in Phase 1 to have a powerful
Phase 2 and 3 (Release) experience. So what happens? Men,
you don't understand your wife's slower response, or why she
is not turned on as quickly as you. You become frustrated and
impatient, wondering why your cold, frigid wife does not start
to heavy-breathe when you try to pull her blouse off, or when
she beholds you in all your unclothed masculine splendor.
Wives, you wonder how this sex-beast could go from the
depths of hardly speaking to you all day to the heights of
passion in under ten seconds!

The second difference is also a matter of time: The husband can move through Phase 2 (Arousal) to Phase 3 (Release/Ejaculation) much faster than his wife. So, before the wife has really even gotten going emotionally or physically, the husband can quickly experience orgasm and be ready to relax, cuddle up (or worse, turn over) and happily go to sleep. The wife feels used, frustrated and unfulfilled. Husbands, you question (silently or aloud) why your wife is such a slowpoke and rarely or never experiences orgasm. You later are completely astonished when your wife's anger, frustration and disappointment make her less responsive the next time you are "in the mood."

Difference number three is a function of frequency: After a man reaches a certain level of excitement in Phase 2 (Arousal), he must go on to Phase 3 (Release/Ejaculation) to be satisfied. Women, however, do not have to have an orgasm during every session of lovemaking to experience contentment, or Phase 4 (Resolution).

Wives who do not understand this physiological and psychological fact about their sexual response can become frustrated by their false expectations. If you think you should experience orgasm every time you make love, you can begin to doubt your sexual capacity or that of your husband.

If you husbands do not understand the nature of your wives' orgasmic frequency, you can put unnecessary pressure upon both of you by trying to bring your wife to climax every time you have intercourse. Or, you can go to the other extreme and give up trying to help your wife have orgasms altogether. The goal should be to allow your wife to enjoy orgasms as often as she is capable, but without a sense of preoccupation or performance. Leave the counting and the comparisons to the talk-show flakes. Focus instead on a loving, mutually satisfying relationship, and you will feel content and connected.

Now let us discuss the issue of frequency from another point of view. A woman can go quite far in showing affection and still not even be thinking of having sexual intercourse. She may be content to cuddle up and feel physically and emotionally close to her husband, and let it go at that. Not so her husband—he usually does not have to go very far into Phase

2 (Arousal/Excitement) before he will need to go through Phase 3 (Release) in order to avoid a frustrating experience.

Husbands and wives need to work very hard to understand one another and meet each other's needs on this critical point. A husband who does not perceive his wife's need for affection and emotional closeness will alienate her and deprive his marriage of the treasure of friendship. Men need to realize that every occasion of affection does not and should not have to end up in "going all the way." As a matter of fact, your wife will resent it if whenever you touch her it is because you want "something else" to happen. She will become leery of any approach you make and will be afraid to warm up to you for fear you will interpret her expressions as an invitation for sex. Conversely, a wife who does not understand the male sexual drive will become critical of her husband. A wife must realize that her husband is more easily aroused than she, and that after a certain point in showing affection, he will need to take matters to their logical conclusion! If not, she will leave him unsatisfied.[2]

Neither the man's nor woman's sexual nature is "right" or "wrong," or "better" or "worse" than the other. What needs to be worked on is our *attitudes*. What is needed is more love, patience, unselfishness and adaptation—from both of us. My guess is that God set it up this way, to call us to develop a character more like his, and to help make life more interesting!

Poor Understanding of Expectation

How many fights, arguments and frustrations have been brought on by unfulfilled or misunderstood expectations? You, O lovely wife, have been feeling romantic all day, and are ready for a wonderful night of love. You prepare his favorite dinner, soak in a luxurious bath, adorn yourself with his favorite evening attire, anoint yourself with those special fragrances, and eagerly await his arrival. He comes home tired, distracted and clueless. He fails to pick up your signals. He retreats behind the newspaper, falls asleep on the couch, or goes out with the guys.

You, O husband, have been in the mood for love since you got that wonderful glimpse of your princess in the shower this morning. You just know it's going to be pure passion tonight! Instead, you encounter a wife who is cranky, weary and ready for an early bedtime—but not so she can play with you! Or, she has planned to have a nice long phone conversation with her mother after the kids are asleep. When she finally does come to bed, she makes her appearance showerless and clothed in burlap. You retreat to the bathroom, draw a tub of cold water, place your passionate but disappointed self therein, and spend an hour reading your Bible.

How do you avoid this? TALK! Don't make your partner be a mind reader. Develop your own special "love language" that you both understand and respond to. Make sure your little hints are heard and grasped. Bring up your needs and desires before leaving home that morning or with a phone call during the day. The higher your expectations, the more urgent it is for you to communicate, because greater will be your disappointment if your expectations are not fulfilled.

Maintaining a healthy, fulfilling sexual relationship is no easy matter. There is not a couple alive who will not encounter problems. However, if you properly identify the problems, get sound advice and counsel, rely on all the resources God gives you, you can deal with them. At different stages of life, the problems will be different. Solve the ones you face now at this stage, and that will prepare you for the next challenge that lies ahead. But whatever you face, never give up on God's plan. In the next chapter we will focus on the positive habits that can foster a romantic marriage, and keep it that way throughout your lives.

CHAPTER 7

The Promise

How delightful is your love,
my sister, my bride!
How much more pleasing
is your love than wine,
and the fragrance of your perfume
than any spice!

SONG OF SONGS 4:10

How do you build a great love life? Here are seven positive steps to take.

Attitude

"Give, and it will be given to you. A good measure, pressed down, shaken together and running over, will be poured into your lap. For with the measure you use, it will be measured to you" (Luke 6:38).

Each of you should look not only to your own interests, but also to the interests of others (Philippians 2:4).

In loving his bride, the church, Jesus did not seek to please himself (Romans 15:3). In marriage, especially in sexual love, we should seek to have this same attitude. If we approach lovemaking with the mindset to draw close, give love, and please our partner, we will be blessed. We will find ourselves aroused and satisfied. Seek to give yourself. Seek to give pleasure. Celebrate and enjoy your marriage. Deep fulfillment awaits you.

Men, you are not there to prove your sexual prowess. You are not there to prove you can turn on your wife and make her multiorgasmic. Women, you are not there to keep up with the latest sexual fads in the women's magazines or to plod your way through another boring night. You are there to give and receive love.

Attention

> Where has your lover gone,
>   most beautiful of women?
> Which way did your lover turn,
>   that we may look for him with you?
> (Song of Songs 6:1).

Notice each other and be attentive at all times. Wives, be sensitive to his need for respect, encouragement and help. Praise him and express your admiration for his good character. Express appreciation for the ways he serves you and the children. Husbands, show concern for her physical, emotional, social and spiritual well-being. Observe the smallest thing she does and let her know what it means to you. Compliment her appearance frequently and sincerely.

Write each other cards or brief notes of thanks, encouragement and appreciation. Surprise each other with small (or large!) gifts. Step in and do an errand or job that has been burdening your spouse. Give those special, knowing looks across a room. In doing these little things every day, and making it a lifetime habit, you are making small deposits into a mutual fund that yields an amazing rate of interest! Sexual intimacy draws its worth and value from these small investments of kindness.

Affection

> Let him kiss me with the kisses of his mouth—
>   for your love is more delightful than wine
> (Song of Songs 1:2).

The kind tenderness of physical touch should permeate a marriage. When it does, the exciting, intimate act of romantic love is a natural next step. Passionate touch is easy and comfortable for such couples, and sexual intimacy is not awkward or clumsy.

Hold hands in public and in private. Sit beside each other. Rest your hand on her hand or your hand on his knee. While sitting, place your arm around her shoulder; when standing put your arm around her waist. Give a light touch on the shoulder when you walk by each other. Snuggle up in his lap. Men, cuddle up with no secret agenda of lovemaking to follow. Hug each other. Learn to give those exquisite, tension-relieving neck and shoulder massages. Even if your hands are not strong, the amazing power of the gentlest human caress can rapturously remove the burdens of a busy day. The same is true of a hand, foot or facial massage. Kiss good morning, good night, good bye, hello and for no reason at all.

All of these actions need to be done in appropriate settings, but my observation is that the vast majority of us err on the side of coolness rather than warmth. I am concerned about and hurt for couples who are rarely seen touching each other. It usually means a corresponding distance in their private love. Why do we leave the hand-holding and the public warmth to unmarried couples? Most of us secretly long for the days when we showed more affection. Well then, change! It is simply a matter of mindfulness and initiative. Couples who do these things reap a rich reward and are the envy of the Distant Majority.

In our previous book, *Raising Awesome Kids in Troubled Times*, I told the story about a conversation I once overheard between my son and a fellow four-year-old in the back of the car. After observing Geri and me giving each other a little kiss of greeting, his friend commented disapprovingly, "Ooooooo....your mommy and daddy *kissed!* *My* mom and dad *never* do that!" David, undaunted, and with great confidence responded, "Well, *my* mom and dad kiss *a lot!*" I would rather have my children know that my wife and I obviously love each other and to observe appropriate affection connected to married love, than to see sex only portrayed as the domain of the unmarried or the adulterous.

Atmosphere

> ...our bed is verdant.
> The beams of our house are cedars;
>   our rafters are firs
> (Song of Songs1:16-17).

The bedroom must be a place of privacy and beauty that provides an atmosphere where sex can be enjoyed. Often it is the shabbiest room in our home. Why? Because we spend all our resources and effort on the rooms that are seen by outsiders. It is also the last room we clean up. "Uhhh, don't go in our room; it's a mess!" is the embarrassed comment we make as we take guests on a tour of our home. It becomes the repository of dirty or unfolded laundry, the ironing board, our checkbook, bills and tax records, and tottering stacks of unread newspapers and magazines. The wallpaper peels, the furniture is Au Tacky, the unsanitized bathroom is generating new life forms, and the closet door is posted with avalanche warnings. To top it all off, the cartoon-character bedsheets borrowed from the kids provide the ultimate inspiration for those unforgettable nights of romantic passion!

Great atmosphere helps produce great sex. Time and care taken to make the bedroom a place of beauty will not return void. Even minimal effort and expense can help. If all your budget allows is a thorough cleaning, then do it! If you can, try a coat of paint, some nice pictures, new sheets, romantic music, candles and other creative touches, and see what happens. Improvement in ambiance could give our love life that extra boost to make it special again.

Attractiveness

> His arms are rods of gold
>   set with chrysolite.
> His body is like polished ivory
>   decorated with sapphires.
> His legs are pillars of marble
>   set on bases of pure gold.
> His appearance is like Lebanon,
>   choice as its cedars
> (Song of Songs 5:14-15).

> How beautiful your sandaled feet,
>   O prince's daughter!
> Your graceful legs are like jewels,
>   the work of a craftsman's hands.
> Your head crowns you like Mount Carmel.
>   Your hair is like royal tapestry;
>   the king is held captive by its tresses.
> (Song of Songs 7:1,5).

We owe it to our partners to look our best and to be physically fit. If you let your body become too heavy or lose its tone, you are degrading the temple of the Holy Spirit (1 Corinthians 6:19) and being inconsiderate of your spouse. You are being selfish and lazy. Stop feeling sorry for yourself. Stop making excuses about metabolism and genetics and get in shape! Quit stalling. God made the human body to respond to exercise and proper diet. For some it may be more of a challenge, but it is a challenge that can and must be successfully overcome. Want to lose weight? Go with Laing's Infallible Weight Loss Miracle Diet: "*Burn up more than you put in.*" Increase your output (exercise!), decrease your input (especially of fatty foods), stick with it, and you will see positive results! If you need to, join a weight-loss group or get help from a medical professional.

Most of us need to tone up our musculature. A flabby, doughy body is not attractive. Simple light exercise done consistently will make a marked difference, both in how you look and how you feel. Feeling good about your appearance has a direct effect on your sexual appetite and confidence. Women are more at peace when they know they look trim, feminine and pretty. Men who are physically fit also have a greater sense of well-being, masculine confidence and sexual motivation.

Attire, Aroma and Allure

> How beautiful you are, my darling!
>   Oh, how beautiful!
>   Your eyes behind your veil are doves.
> Your hair is like a flock of goats...
> (Song of Songs 4:1).

Your lips are like a scarlet ribbon;
    your mouth is lovely
(Song of Songs 4:3a).

Your two breasts are like two fawns, like twin fawns...
(Song of Songs 4:5a).

You have stolen my heart, my sister, my bride;
    you have stolen my heart
with one glance of your eyes,
    with one jewel of your necklace.
How delightful is your love, my sister, my bride!
    How much more pleasing is your love than wine,
    and the fragrance of your perfume than any spice!
Your lips drop sweetness as the honeycomb, my bride;
    milk and honey are under your tongue...
(Song of Songs 4:9-11).

I have taken off my robe—
    must I put it on again?
I have washed my feet—
    must I soil them again?
My lover thrust his hand through the latch-opening;
    my heart began to pound for him.
I arose to open for my lover,
    and my hands dripped with myrrh,
my fingers with flowing myrrh,
    on the handles of the lock
(Song of Songs 5:3-5).

These passages show that the woman's clothing, appearance and aroma aroused the passion of her husband, her lover. The sight and thought of her excited him. She looked alluring. He knew she would look beautiful when he came to her. She knew she looked wonderful, and thus, she felt like making love. She wore jewelry, a beautiful robe, an alluring veil, makeup, had her hair styled attractively, was refreshingly clean, and used the finest of fragrances in generous amounts. (See also Song of Songs 6:7.) Christian women can learn much from Solomon's wife about making themselves attractive to their husbands. Certainly in real life, every night together cannot be the ideal, but this passage reminds women not to forget the importance of sexual attraction in marriage. It also reminds them to set up certain nights as romantically special and not to fall into a humdrum pattern in their love lives.

Some women are still wearing their high school pajamas to bed. These things are gross, dingy and pilled. No matter that they are warm and comfortable—they ought to be consigned to the garbage can. Most men want something a bit more exciting than the long-sleeved ankle-length flannel Evening Wear by Nuns outfits that some of you have been wearing. Ask your husband what he likes. Surely you can agree on some bedtime attire that he thinks looks sexy and that also makes you feel sexy!

Use perfume. The kind he likes. All over. Lots of it. Enough to set the room on fire. Be absolutely fresh and clean for lovemaking. Floss. Brush your teeth. Not just that morning! Right before bed, please! Fix up your hair. Put on lipstick if he likes it. Look as good (in a different wardrobe, of course!) as if you were going out for a nice evening.

Husbands, there will have to be some money shelled out for this. Don't grumble about your wife's appearance if you make her feel like a spendthrift every time she brings home something new to wear. And this not only includes evening attire, but the clothing she needs to look up-to-date and attractive every day.

My lover is radiant and ruddy,
  outstanding among ten thousand.
His head is purest gold;
  his hair is wavy
  and black as a raven.
His eyes are like doves
  by the water streams,
  washed in milk,
  mounted like jewels.
His cheeks are like beds of spice
  yielding perfume.
His lips are like lilies
  dripping with myrrh.
His arms are rods of gold
  set with chrysolite.

His body is like polished ivory
  decorated with sapphires.
His legs are pillars of marble
  set on bases of pure gold.
His appearance is like Lebanon,
  choice as its cedars
His mouth is sweetness itself;
  he is altogether lovely.
This is my lover, this my friend,
  O daughters of Jerusalem
(Song of Songs 5:10-16).

This man looked handsome and smelled great. Men, wear what your wife likes! Let her help in selecting all of your clothing, including what you wear to bed. Most men need help in knowing how to dress in styles and colors that enhance their appearance. Take a shower. Right before bed. Use soap. Scrub well. Everywhere. You too need to floss and brush. Especially shave off the stubbly day-old beard. Use deodorant and cologne.

Go through your clothing and get rid of your graying, gross underwear. Make it a practice to look sharp when you go out. Don't look and act like a slob around the house. The fact that you are married does not give you the right to engage in locker-room behavior within eyesight or earshot of your wife. It turns her off when you do the gross things that you did when you were a kid or that all your high school buddies used to laugh about.

Articulation

How beautiful you are and how pleasing,
  O love, with your delights!
(Song of Songs 7:6).

Talk to each other about your love life. Ask your spouse "What pleases you?" Observe what stimulates them, but also encourage them to say it. There must develop between husband and wife a comfortableness in discussing sexual things. Otherwise, we may go for months or even years in ignorance about what is pleasing or displeasing to our partners. It could be something about hygiene, attire or about actual physical actions of lovemaking; whatever it is, we simply *must* learn to be open in discussion. We should communicate both the positives and the negatives, always in an intimate, gentle manner. Women, you in particular need to clearly let your husbands know of the changes that may occur in your body's sensitivity and responsiveness.

Express your attraction and your love. Tell what it is about your spouse that stimulates you, and let him or her know the physical, verbal, visual and emotional things that make your love life thrilling. It may be a laugh, a smile, a way of standing, a tone of voice—usually something that they are unaware of, but will be pleased to learn. The lovers in Song of Songs described in beautiful terms their delight in each other's bodies: hair, eyes, cheeks, neck, lips, tongue, teeth, breath, breasts and waistline—all of these are described in glowing and poetic terms to one another. This in itself provides immeasurable stimulation and intensity to lovemaking, and is one of the secrets of truly exciting sex.

Both people should feel physically and conscientiously comfortable with what is done in making love. If either of you feels embarrassed or has qualms of conscience, then it is time to talk and work things out. You should never pressure your spouse to do anything during lovemaking that offends his or her scruples or that makes them feel ashamed or dirty. A more modest partner should not be subjected to ridicule or be made to feel ignorant and unenlightened, but should be treated with respect and consideration.

Having said this, let me say that the scriptural emphasis seems to me to be upon freedom and creativity in married love, and not on limitations. Your bodies belong to each other (1 Corinthians 7:4) and should be given to one another in totality. Some of us, because of past sins or misunderstanding of the Scriptures, have unnecessarily limited the joy and celebration that should be present in our lovemaking. This should be talked about between yourselves, or with the help of competent advisors. For those who are overmodest, I would suggest a careful study of the biblical passages on the subject, with a special emphasis on Song of

Songs. Besides the passages already quoted in this chapter, consider these:

> You are a garden locked up, my sister, my bride;
>   you are a spring enclosed, a sealed fountain.
> Your plants are an orchard of pomegranates
>   with choice fruits,
>   with henna and nard,
>   nard and saffron,
>   calamus and cinnamon,
>   with every kind of incense tree,
>   with myrrh and aloes
>   and all the finest spices.
> You are a garden fountain,
>   a well of flowing water
>   streaming down from Lebanon.
> Awake, north wind,
>   and come, south wind!
> Blow on my garden,
>   that its fragrance may spread abroad.
> Let my lover come into his garden
>   and taste its choice fruits.
> I have come into my garden, my sister, my bride;
>   I have gathered my myrrh with my spice.
> I have eaten my honeycomb and my honey;
>   I have drunk my wine and my milk.
> Eat, O friends, and drink;
>   drink your fill, O lovers
> (Song of Songs 4:12-5:1).

> Your stature is like that of the palm,
>   and your breasts like clusters of fruit.
> I said, "I will climb the palm tree;
>   I will take hold of its fruit."
> May your breasts be like the clusters of the vine,
>   the fragrance of your breath like apples,
>   and your mouth like the best wine
> (Song of Songs 7:7-9).

The consideration of matters like oral sex, creative or varied coital positions, and stimulation of different areas of the anatomy are in my judgment best left up to each couple within the privacy of their own bedroom. On the foundation of marital sexual freedom, with love and consideration for each other's feelings and tastes, everything can be worked out to a mutually satisfactory end that leaves us with an ever changing, ever growing sexual love that only gets better through the years.

Romantic love is a wonderful gift. It has been designed by God to be a glorious, joyful and satisfying experience in every marriage. When it is present, married life, and all of life, takes on a cheerful and happy air along with a sense of fun and celebration. We, as friends and lovers, are filled with satisfaction, contentment and delight. That is the glorious plan of God!

One More Thought...

The sexual relationship between a husband and wife is of tremendous importance in a healthy, strong and lasting marriage. I know that it has been said, but let me emphasize it again: The thing that distinguishes the relationship of husband and wife from every other relationship in life is the "one flesh" aspect. I believe it is what Paul refers to as the "mystery" in marriage (Ephesians 5:32). Sexual intimacy in marriage, when practiced regularly and unselfishly, provides just that—intimacy. It causes both husband and wife to feel close and secure. Take it out, and the depth of closeness and love for one another will not reach its God-given potential.

In most marriages, one of the great challenges is bringing two people with different sexual drives together in a mutually satisfying way. Usually (but not always) it is the wife who is less desirous of frequent sex. If this is so in your case, you must deal with it. You must grasp how much your lack of enthusiasm for sex is hurting your marriage. Not only do you need the closeness and release more than you realize, but you may also be setting your spouse up for serious struggles and temptations with lust and other sexual sins. No man wants to be repeatedly rejected, whether it be by outright refusal or by consistent disinterest. If rejection of any type continues, many men will stop trying to initiate lovemaking. Others will become obviously resentful and angry, and still others will quietly harden their hearts and distance themselves emotionally from their wives.

Women, you must deal with whatever it is that is keeping you from enjoying a regular sexual relationship. For some of you it is selfishness and laziness. You are wrapped up in your own life, your job or your children, and your marriage—especially romance—has a very low priority. For others, it is something as simple (but damaging) as your appearance. You are overweight and feel unattractive and unsexy. A woman who is embarrassed by her appearance cannot relax and enjoy an intimate and vulnerable sexual relationship. From working with many women over the years, I have learned that no one loses weight successfully and permanently until they deeply want to do it in their own heart. But realize this: By your refusal to overcome your problem you are hurting every other relationship in your life, most especially your marriage. Decide to lose weight, get in shape, and fix yourself up. Not only will you live longer, but life will be better in every way!

Sam and I both know how difficult it is to stay in shape. As we have gotten older we have had to become more serious than ever about keeping the weight off and staying fit. It takes time, effort and sacrifice, but we do it for each other, for ourselves and for the sake of our example and effectiveness.

Let me conclude with a few words to husbands. Please understand that if the only time you become truly attentive, affectionate and loving is when you are "in the mood for love," you are *killing* your sexual relationship with your wife. In fact, you may find her becoming more and more distant from you because you construe any display of affection and warmth from her as a sexual overture. Just as men need sex to be close, women need to feel close to have sex. Husbands, women want and need to be loved, hugged, touched and caressed at times purely because you care for them—with "no strings attached." Some of you would be amazed at the complete turnaround in your wife's response to you both emotionally and sexually if you would simply, but genuinely, express love for her.

Sexual love is a great gift of God to be enjoyed and cherished for a lifetime. While the passion and excitement of a new marriage is a tremendous joy and a memory to be cherished forever, nothing can compare to a love that has been enjoyed and practiced for a very long time. A marriage that continues to grow over the years will experience a sexual union that continues to reach greater heights of enjoyment and deeper levels of satisfaction. This ever-increasing fulfillment is available to *all* who have given themselves unreservedly to their spouses in marriage. Enjoy and celebrate your life together!

Now it is time to put this book down for the night. You have better things to do!

Geri Laing

PART

3

·Reality·

CHAPTER 8

It's Only Money

"But seek first his kingdom and
his righteousness, and all these things
will be given to you as well."

MATTHEW 6:33

M oney should be a blessing, not a curse. As I see it in the
Scriptures, there are three reasons God gives us material blessings. First, he gives them to us to sustain our lives
and the lives of our children. Second, he gives us money that
it may be used to advance his kingdom. And last, he gives us
our financial resources that we might help the poor and practice hospitality. All of these are good and righteous purposes.
The Bible further teaches us that every blessing we have comes
from God (James 1:17) and that everything God created is
good (1 Timothy 4:4) and should be used for his glory.

Why is it that something God intends to be a blessing
becomes a problem in our marriages? Our attitude is typically
the problem. As there are three proper uses of money, there
are three wrong attitudes about it.

First, the love of money is wrong.

> For the love of money is a root of all kinds of evil. Some
> people, eager for money, have wandered from the faith
> and pierced themselves with many griefs (1 Timothy 6:10).

Money itself is not wrong—it is *living* for money and the
love of money that is wrong.

Second, money becomes a problem when it becomes a
source of division and conflict. Arguments over money and

the budget are some of the most commonplace and destructive in marriage. Disagreement on money matters can drive marriages apart and create continual tension.

Third, money becomes a problem when it is a source of anxiety. Worry about paying the bills, buying a home, taking care of the children's college education, etc., can become such a burden that it creates constant pressure in marriage.

But all these attitudes can change! I want to share with you ten attitudes that can revolutionize your thinking about money and can make it a blessing instead of a curse.

Attitudes Toward Finances

1. Establish the Right Priorities

In the theme scripture of this chapter, Jesus tells us that we should seek first his kingdom and his righteousness and that when we do, all of our other needs will be met. Our first priority in life is not to make money or to pay the bills, but to serve God and advance his kingdom. When God sees that we have an attitude of putting him first, he moves powerfully to sustain and support us in living the life-style of a disciple.

Jesus declares that we must choose between God and money:

> "No one can serve two masters. Either he will hate the one and love the other, or he will be devoted to the one and despise the other. You cannot serve both God and Money" (Matthew 6:24).

A married couple must decide once for all that God will come above everything else, including material possessions. When we do this, it removes anxiety about money from our lives. Most people I know who worry about money have either placed too great a value upon it or have little faith in God.

> Do not wear yourself out to get rich;
>   have the wisdom to show restraint.
> Cast but a glance at riches, and they are gone,
>   for they will surely sprout wings
>   and fly off to the sky like an eagle
> (Proverbs 23:4-5).

2. Live Within Your Means

> Do not be a man who strikes hands in pledge
>   or puts up security for debts;
> if you lack the means to pay,
>   your very bed will be snatched from under you
> (Proverbs 22:26-27).
>
> Finish your outdoor work
>   and get your fields ready;
>   after that, build your house
> (Proverbs 24:27).

We should live happily and thankfully within the life-style that our income will support. The apostle Paul addresses this issue:

> I am not saying this because I am in need, for I have learned to be content whatever the circumstances. I know what it is to be in need, and I know what it is to have plenty. I have learned the secret of being content in any and every situation, whether well fed or hungry, whether living in plenty or in want. I can do everything through him who gives me strength (Philippians 4:11-13).

Many of us need to learn the lesson of contentment. Paul was content whether he had much or little. If God has blessed you with an abundance, be grateful—don't feel guilty! Use your abundance to bless God's kingdom and the lives of God's people, and to meet the needs of the poor. If you have less, do not worry or be envious of those who have more. Work hard to advance your situation, but do not allow yourself to be robbed of gratitude and contentment. So many married couples feel that they would be happy if they only had more money. The truth is, joy and happiness do not depend on how much we have, but on how close we are to God.

Living within your means is especially important for young couples just starting out in married life. The temptation for you is to want to have immediately the car, the home and the furniture that your parents worked all their lives to accumulate. In many cases, your parents had to work, suffer and sweat to earn what they have, and you need to realize this and be patient.

There is something special about starting out with virtually nothing (and it sure gives you some great stories to tell the kids later on!). Geri and I weren't exactly loaded when we got married. We went on our honeymoon in the heat of the summer in a 1969 Volkswagen bug with no air-conditioning. We came back to a one-bedroom apartment and barely any furniture. We scrimped to buy a bed. We ate at a card table. I remember making the stand for our small black and white television by covering a pasteboard box with contact paper. Our easy chair was a nice pillow we threw out on the living room floor. For our six-month anniversary, we pooled our funds and split a sandwich and each had a side order at our favorite lunch spot. Our second car was an oil-burning environmental disaster of a station wagon that Geri's parents graciously sold us for one dollar. (We later sold it for a profit— twenty-five bucks!) Some college students in our campus ministry group had mercy on us because we could not afford a Christmas tree. When they went on Christmas break they took theirs down, brought it over to our apartment and set it up for us, decorations and all!

These are some of our most precious memories. We remember being deeply in love and having the time of our lives! We remember having a great marriage and being thankful that we had each other, God's blessing and God's people all around us. We lived within our means and were able to gradually build up our financial resources. We did not make ourselves miserable by wishing we had more.

We must continue to live within our means even after we have children. We can look around and see the nice clothing other people's children are wearing and become embarrassed. We see the bicycles, video games and toys that others may lavish on their kids, and we begin to feel that our children cannot be happy unless they have these things, too. What a terrible mistake! What a horrible lesson we are teaching our children! We can find ways for our kids to be well-dressed and have the things they need and still live within our means. The mistake we make is trying to be more than we are and having a worldly, competitive attitude about how we evaluate our worth and the worth of others.

3. Design and Stick with a Budget

> Commit to the LORD whatever you do,
>   and your plans will succeed
> (Proverbs 16:3).

Sit down and calculate your monthly income and your best estimate of your monthly expenses. Put it all on paper. Come up with a plan by which you can make the payments in a timely, organized fashion. If you do not know what your monthly income and expenses are, you are headed for disaster. *Never* spend outside your budget unless both of you have talked it over and are in complete agreement. Making a budget is an activity that both of you should do together and that both must understand.

(More on this in the next section of the chapter.)

4. Put God's Work First in Your Budget

Under the Old Covenant, families were expected to give a tithe (a tenth) of their income to God's work.

> "Will a man rob God? Yet you rob me.
> "But you ask, 'How do we rob you?'
> "In tithes and offerings. You are under a curse—the whole nation of you—because you are robbing me. Bring the whole tithe into the storehouse, that there may be food in my house. Test me in this," says the LORD Almighty, "and see if I will not throw open the floodgates of heaven and pour out so much blessing that you will not have room enough for it. I will prevent pests from devouring your crops, and the vines in your fields will not cast their fruit," says the LORD Almighty. "Then all the nations will call you blessed, for yours will be a delightful land," says the LORD Almighty (Malachi 3:8-12). (See also Numbers 18:21; Leviticus 27:30.)

Further study of the Old Testament shows that there were other offerings given by the Jews throughout the year that meant their total giving was probably double the tithe. In the teachings of Jesus there is no set number or percentage given, but my own conviction is that the ten-percent figure is the place to start, and then we need the faith that we can go higher.

In the early church they went far beyond ten percent in meeting the needs of God's people and God's kingdom (2 Corinthians 8-9). The work of God's kingdom depends upon our weekly support, and we should be openhearted and generous in the way we approach this need. It is my observation that couples who love God's kingdom and put it first in their giving and who are disciplined and generous in their offerings are blessed financially. Above all, they are blessed spiritually as they return to God some of what he has given to them.

5. Avoid Credit Buying

> The rich rule over the poor,
> and the borrower is servant to the lender
> (Proverbs 22:7).

I remember that shortly before graduating from college I began to receive numerous invitations from credit card companies to get on their bandwagon. I said to myself, "Sam, you must be a pretty sharp guy since all of these banks and companies want you to be a part of their organization and have one of their nice credit cards." How wrong I was! I signed up. We did not use the card for many months, but then we had a major car repair bill, and I put it on the credit card. We could not pay off the balance immediately, and we began paying the minimum payment. Then we began to think that we needed other things and began to use the card to purchase gifts and other small items. Before long, the balance was up over a thousand dollars. We realized our mistake, cut the credit card into pieces and paid it off. I will never forget the relief we felt when we sent in that check!

Do not fall into the credit-card trap! It seems harmless and painless to lay a piece of plastic on the counter when we buy something. "It's such a small purchase," we think. "We'll pay it off in just a few days." But then we do not pay it off because of the pressure of other challenges in our budget. We run that card to its limit, then we get another and we do the same, then another and another. Soon we have thousands of dollars at high interest rates eating away our financial resources.

If you must use credit cards, I recommend using only those that require the balance to be paid off every month. If you use a gasoline credit card, pay it off every month. If you use any other credit card, pay it off every month. If you do not have the discipline to do this, then cut up your cards.

What about purchasing a home or an automobile on credit? For most of us, this is the only way we will be able to make these large purchases, especially in the early years of our marriage. There is nothing wrong with making larger purchases on credit, if we have adequately budgeted in the payments. Before making such a commitment, figure out your limit on the monthly payment and do not go above it, no matter what. This is especially true in purchasing cars. Many young couples go out and buy a high-priced automobile at a high interest rate. It ends up limiting their ability to do anything else financially for years. It may be better that you delay in buying a home or a new car until you can save a larger amount for the down payment. If that is the case, then so be it. It is better to wait for a few months (or years) so that when you make the purchase it does not become the controlling factor in your budget and attitude.

6. Pay Bills on Time

> Let no debt remain outstanding, except the continuing debt to love one another, for he who loves his fellowman has fulfilled the law (Romans 13:8).

Whether we are paying our monthly bills or paying off loans, we are under obligation to pay on time. Too many of us are willing to send in payments late saying, "Well, they really don't want the money until they send the second notice." This is unfair, undisciplined and a poor example. Pay your bills on time! When you apply for a home mortgage, your credit will be carefully checked, and if you have a record of late payments, it could cause your application to be rejected. Be diligent, even in paying off smaller loans of a few dollars. Some of us have a number of small loans from friends in the $10 to $100 range and are thinking, "Oh, I'll pay it off when I get around to it." The fact is that we are taking advantage of the generosity and love of our friends and tempting them to have bad attitudes toward us.

The same is true for larger loans from friends and family. Any loans you receive of this nature should be made with a clear understanding of how it will be paid back. It should be written down on paper and signed. This may seem cold and impersonal, but you are actually protecting the relationship. How many close relationships have been harmed by a misunderstanding and disagreement on the repayment of a personal loan? It may be wise never to borrow money from family and friends. We can end up relying on the hard work and industry of others rather than on our own efforts in building a financial base. There is nothing like the feeling of knowing that you have worked hard for what you have!

7. Listen to Advice

> The way of a fool seems right to him,
>   but a wise man listens to advice
> (Proverbs 12:15).
>
> Pride only breeds quarrels,
>   but wisdom is found in those who take advice
> (Proverbs 13:10).
>
> Listen to advice and accept instruction,
>   and in the end you will be wise
> (Proverbs 19:20).

The scriptures above tell us clearly that we need to listen to others as we live our lives. In no area is openness more important than in finances. Many couples have gotten themselves into financial trouble because they fancied themselves financial wizards. In my experience, some of the people who have had the most confidence about how to invest and earn money have made some of the most foolish mistakes. You should seek advice in two primary areas.

First, you need to listen to your spouse. It is a terrible mistake for one marriage partner to make all of the decisions about money. Even if that person is more gifted and effective in managing the finances, it is a mistake for him or her to do it alone. Their intellectual ability may not be equal in strength to their spirituality, and they may make bad priority decisions. Second, the other spouse needs to understand why, how and where the money is being spent and be in agreement. Without this the marriage is headed for disagreement and difficulty. One person may carry the load of organizing the budget and setting things up, but the other person *must* have an understanding and appreciation of what is happening. When both have been involved, financial challenges or difficulties will not bring the temptation to lose confidence or to have a bad attitude.

The second group of people from whom we need advice are wise, mature friends. Geri and I have always made it our practice to seek the counsel of spiritually and financially capable friends before we make any major financial commitment. Whether buying a house, a car or making a decision about our children's education, we always seek advice before making any moves. This practice has brought God's blessing and has saved us from many foolish decisions.

If you want to run the finances without input from your spouse, my question for you is "What are you trying to hide?" My second question is "Just how smart do you think you are?" If, as a couple, you do not want anyone else involved in your financial decisions, I ask you the same two questions. It takes humility to open up our lives for the viewing and comment of others, but the rewards are immense. There are many couples today who wish they had sought or listened to advice in financial matters. They now live under a crushing burden of debt and would give anything if they could turn back the hands of time. I urge you— don't repeat their mistake!

8. *Work Hard and Build a Solid Financial Base*

> A sluggard does not plow in season;
> > so at harvest time he looks but finds nothing
> (Proverbs 20:4).

Do you see a man skilled in his work?
    He will serve before kings;
    he will not serve before obscure men
(Proverbs 22:29).

He who works his land will have abundant food,
    but the one who chases fantasies
    will have his fill of poverty
(Proverbs 28:19).

Dishonest money dwindles away,
    but he who gathers money little by little makes it grow
(Proverbs 13:11).

The Bible teaches us that the way to financial success is
plain, prosaic hard work. There are no short cuts. Find a career track, and stick with it. Work hard to improve yourself.
Acquire a skill, and you will be valuable to an employer. If
you desire to build your own business, do use caution and
get advice lest you commit yourself to an undertaking that
requires you to work a schedule that leaves you little time for
other godly commitments. But if you decide it is the right
move, then be prepared for the hard work and sacrifice that
will be necessary.

So many people are waiting for the lottery numbers to
come up right or for their rich old uncle to die and leave them
a fortune. These things will probably never happen, and even
if they do, hard work and discipline are still the means by
which you will keep whatever may be given you.

I am distressed at how many people work beneath their
potential. I see college graduates working in fast-food res-
taurants because they are too lazy to get out and try to find
work. I have seen others drop out before graduation because
they simply lack the willpower to stay in school to the end.
I see other people who could equip themselves to earn more
by enrolling in night classes and learning a skill, but who are
too unmotivated, lazy and undisciplined to make the effort.
I see too many men and women in lower-level positions in
their companies when a bit of initiative and self-improve-
ment would take them much higher. Certainly we should
not pour all of our efforts into worldly success. But I believe

we owe it to God to be our best. It speaks worlds about our commitment to Christ when we conduct ourselves in this manner. We earn the respect of others, of ourselves and of our spouses when we are hard workers. How many marriages suffer from tensions brought on by the fact that one spouse is not working hard enough, is an underachiever and is not bringing in the kind of financial support he or she is capable of?

The Bible teaches us that those who want to get rich fall into a trap (1 Timothy 6:9), but there is everything right about working hard so you can support yourself and your family and so you can help others who are in need (Ephesians 4:28; 1 Thessalonians 4:11-12).

9. Set Aside Some of Your Income in a Savings Account

Wisdom dictates that we should save some of our income on a regular basis to help us deal with special and unexpected needs, both in our lives and in the lives of others. Start saving now for your children's college education and for your retirement. A savings account provides a cushion for the unexpected, keeps us off the edge of financial disaster, and gives us more financial freedom. Another reason to have a savings account is to prepare ourselves in advance for upcoming required expenses such as insurance payments, taxes or other bills that occur less than monthly. If you learn to save in advance, then these payments will not put you under stress when they are due. I recommend setting up automatic savings deposits every pay period in cooperation with your bank. This ensures that you save the money and that it is done in a timely, disciplined manner.

Some people feel that it is faithless to build a savings account. "Why not just live from day to day? Doesn't God take care of us that way?" It is true that we should live one day at a time trusting God for our daily needs, but we need to remember that God expects us to be good stewards of what he gives us. He even uses the example of the industrious ant, who works hard and lays aside his provisions in advance, as a rebuke to our lack of forethought and discipline (Proverbs 6:6-8). Besides, many of us have been thankful for those who had the money saved and used it to help us at definite points of need in our lives. If no one saved, who would help in such times?

10. Be Generous

> A stingy man is eager to get rich
> and is unaware that poverty awaits him
> (Proverbs 28:22).

> He who gives to the poor will lack nothing,
> but he who closes his eyes to them receives many curses
> (Proverbs 28:27).

> One man gives freely, yet gains even more;
> another withholds unduly, but comes to poverty.
> A generous man will prosper;
> he who refreshes others will himself be refreshed
> (Proverbs 11:24-25).

An attitude of generous openhandedness with what we have is a beautiful thing. The Bible teaches us that God gives generously, even to those who do not appreciate or understand it (Matthew 5:45). We should cultivate an attitude of generosity and giving in our everyday lives. If we are always worrying about how much things cost and begrudging what we do for others, it makes us unattractive people:

> Do not eat the food of a stingy man,
> do not crave his delicacies;
> for he is the kind of man
> who is always thinking about the cost.
> "Eat and drink," he says to you,
> but his heart is not with you
> (Proverbs 23:6-7).

Some of us are stingy in what we give to our spouses and our marriages. We won't buy a nice birthday gift or anniversary present, or surprise our mates with something we purchase spontaneously. We excuse ourselves by saying, "Oh, those are just material things." What we must realize is that gifts are a way to express love. Jesus appreciated and affirmed such an expression even when his disciples thought it was a waste (Matthew 26:8-13). Be generous and giving in your marriage!

Others of us are not hospitable and warm to others because we are always worried about how much we are spending. We are the last ones to offer to pick up the tab for dinner. When we have people over, we do not make the special effort to show we care by what we serve or the effort we make. I am not saying that we need to become big spenders in order to make friends, but there is a time to sacrifice and give nice gifts to show special attention.

Another vital area for generosity is in giving to the needy. The Bible is replete with examples and teachings about helping those who are less fortunate. "He who is kind to the poor lends to the Lord, and he will reward him for what he has done" (Proverbs 19:17). All around us are people who have needs. We can get involved by helping the poor directly with our own gifts or by working for and financially supporting organizations that alleviate their sufferings.

Ten Steps to Financial Freedom

Now we want to discuss the practical steps to take to get yourselves organized on a budget. If you are discouraged in your family finances, there is hope. Use the ten steps that follow as practical help in getting out of trouble and onto solid ground:

1. What is your total income each month?

It is important that you understand exactly what you are bringing in. If your income is variable because you are in a profession such as commission sales, make your best conservative estimate. What time of the month will it come in? Write all of the dates and figures down.

2. What are your fixed expenses each month?

Be sure to find all of them. First, put down the amount of your present weekly offering, then move on to your rent or mortgage. Make an estimate of variable monthly bills such as utilities, including electric, gas, telephone, water, sewer, etc. Include your car payment and credit-card payments. In calculating credit-card payments, record your total balance owed and the minimum acceptable monthly payment for each card. Include any payments you are making to pay off personal loans. Be sure to include your quarterly (or other less-than-monthly) payments and when they are due.

3. What are the variable expenses you can standardize?

Working with your spouse, make your best estimate on such monthly expenses as food, clothing, laundry, personal care and personal spending, including entertainment and gifts. Note: The grocery budget will probably be higher than you think! Make your best estimate—it can later be adjusted.

4. Put a rough budget together.

Group the bills into two categories: those due the first half of the month and then those due the second half. Write them down on an accounting spreadsheet. Be sure to include your quarterly and biyearly payments into monthly "payments" that you will need to be saving for in advance. Both husband and wife should be given a cash allowance as a part of the family budget. For example, if the wife does the grocery shopping, she needs to be given the cash amount of the food budget. This money is hers to use as she sees fit. If she is frugal, the extra money is hers to use in other ways. Included in her allotment would be other items such as laundry, expenses for the children, etc. (It may be wise for her to divide the cash into envelopes marked for each budget item.)

The husband also needs his personal allotment. This would include his money for any personal spending (meals out, entertainment, gifts, etc.). The idea behind giving the husband and wife a standard allotment is to give both more freedom to manage their own funds and the responsibility to manage a personal budget. This is far better than continually asking the spouse in charge of the checkbook for money every few days. Using this plan, neither husband nor wife can spend more than their allotted budget unless both discuss it and agree. Once they have spent their allotted budget, their spending is over for the month unless a joint decision is made.

5. Get things under control.

Credit cards. As we said earlier, credit-card spending must be controlled or eliminated.

ATM visits. Automatic teller machines are a wonderful invention that enable us to have more convenience in our daily lives. However, their convenience can backfire on us. We can develop the dangerous habit of dropping by the bank and withdrawing small amounts of money to sustain us from day to day. This results in unorganized, undisciplined spending that depletes our budget and wreaks havoc in our organization. No unplanned visits to the ATM machine allowed! (Frankly, some individuals and couples are so undisciplined that they should not even possess an ATM card because of the temptation of abuse.)

Budget allotments. Make yourself a rule that both of you get your allotted funds on a set calendar basis. (Let me reiterate once again: no out-of-budget spending unless both partners approve!)

6. Five strategies for attacking debt

Pay off smaller bills first. Why do this? First, it clears up your account sheet and makes things simpler. Second, it is very encouraging to see bills totally paid off. Third, the money that is freed up can be applied to paying off other bills.

Here is how it works: You have three credit cards, one has a balance of $100, another $800 and another $1,500. Pay the minimum amount on the cards with large debt, and put more money into paying off the smallest one quickly. When it is paid in full, take the monthly amount used to pay off that card, and add it to the amount you were paying on the next higher one. Repeat the process until all cards are paid in full. It may be wiser for you to tackle this problem another way, particularly if some of these cards have extremely high interest rates, but I have found that this has helped me (and others) to quickly get on top of the budget in the most encouraging manner.

Reduce your variable or optional expenses. If, after calculating your budget, you find that it is too tight or you are still in the red, then you have to reduce expenses. This can mean cutting off cable TV, the newspaper subscription, the health club or other extraneous items. Some things may not need to be completely eliminated but just trimmed back. These decisions should be made by husband and wife together.

Increase income. There are ways that you can bring in more money. Perhaps older children can work part time or the wife (if she is not working already) can bring in some extra income. My greatest concern here is that if mothers are away from young children it may not be the best choice spiritually for the family in the long term. Also, the expense of childcare can make outside work unprofitable. So before this option is chosen, be sure that it is talked over with wise advisors!

Loan consolidation. It may be helpful to group several smaller bills into one larger one by means of loan consolidation. Be sure that the interest rate of the new loan is in your favor.

Radical steps. It may be that your expenses are far above your realistic expectations of income. This means that you may have to sell a car, sell your home or move into an apartment with less expensive rent. These are steps we must be willing to take if they will make the difference in getting our heads above water. Rather than borrowing money or compromising our involvement in God's kingdom by taking an extra job, it may be better to scale back our life-style. We must be willing to do whatever we need to do to become financially responsible. These kinds of moves should be made only after talking with your spouse and listening to wise, spiritual counsel.

7. *Get your contribution in order.*

We have already spoken about how God's kingdom needs to come first in our financial life. A great place to start in our weekly giving is at ten percent of our gross income. If you are not presently capable of doing this, then do the best you can. The principles behind giving are that we give out of our own conviction (2 Corinthians 8:3-4) and we do it with a cheerful heart (2 Corinthians 9:7). Others cannot make the decision for us, but they can advise us. You must make this decision before God, and feel resolved about what you have done. I would also urge that you plan carefully and save money on a regular basis for any special needs such as helping the needy, helping with mission work or other financial opportunities that may arise in God's kingdom. Pay close attention to the plans laid out in your congregation so you will not be unprepared when the time comes for special giving.

8. Set up a savings account.

Set up a savings account and make consistent contributions to it. As I said earlier, I recommend an automatic monthly withdrawal by the bank for your savings. Even if it is a small amount, you will be surprised and pleased at how quickly it adds up. And you will be happy the next time there is an unexpected expense and you can cover it out of your savings without destroying your monthly cash flow.

9. Decide who will manage the checkbook.

One of you is probably better at managing the checkbook than the other. In the early years of our marriage, I developed our budgets and handled the checkbook myself. I was capable, but I took a longer time to figure it all out and tended to be shortsighted. Now Geri manages our checkbook. She is proficient at keeping up with the bills and is especially good at building our savings. If I ever sense that the financial pressures are becoming too heavy for her, we sit down, talk and make sure that our budget is still realistic. We always work together. The partner who is not involved in keeping the checkbook is responsible for knowing what is going on with the finances. It is a terrible mistake to simply turn over total responsibility to one spouse because it is unfair to him or her and leaves the other open for bad attitudes.

10. Get others involved in your financial life.

I have already made the case for letting other people help with financial decisions. Do this on a regular basis. If you are feeling money pressures, let your closest Christian friends know about it, and ask for their advice. If you need more expert help, there are people in God's kingdom who are spiritually minded and who are trained in financial management. Find out who they are and ask if they can help you. But remember, for some people, this is their job, and they may need to charge something for their services.

⁘

We began by saying that money should be a blessing and not a curse. If you develop godly attitudes about your finances and take the practical advice given in this chapter, you will experience the blessing of financial solidity and have less temptation to worry. You will also avoid strains in your marriage. Take no short cuts, work together, put God first, and you will see God's blessing upon all that you have!

CHAPTER 9

Peace Accord

> But the wisdom that comes from
> heaven is first of all pure; then
> peace-loving, considerate,
> submissive, full of mercy and good
> fruit, impartial and sincere.
> Peacemakers who sow in peace raise
> a harvest of righteousness.
>
> JAMES 3:17-18

A peaceful, harmonious marriage is a great blessing from God. To be deeply in love and to be at peace with one another means that we are enjoying the promised benefits of our union. Peace in marriage is not intended only for a select few—it is what God wants all of us to enjoy. It is something that we must seek, treasure and work for. It is something that we must expect and never be satisfied until we obtain.

On the other hand, we must recognize that conflict in marriage is inevitable. Indeed, the Scriptures teach that conflict can bring about a greater good. Differences with our husband or wife can cause us to examine ourselves and deepen our relationship: "As iron sharpens iron, so one man sharpens another" (Proverbs 27:17). After undergoing a difficult time of conflict, couples may find that they have forged an even stronger bond.

But none of us wants a marriage of continual conflict. Conflict should be an occasional event and not a consistent pattern. Constant quarreling, arguing and fighting can ruin what should be the happiness and joy of friendship: "Better a

135

dry crust with peace and quiet than a house full of feasting, with strife (Proverbs 17:1). God does not intend marriage to be a long ordeal of tension. Continual disagreement can ultimately destroy a marriage and will also destroy the happiness of our children.

In this chapter we seek to explain the *causes* of conflict so that we can understand and avoid them. Second, we will discuss the *cure* of conflict—how we can overcome the inevitable differences that will arise between us.

Causes of Conflict

A Prideful Attitude

"Pride only breeds quarrels, but wisdom is found in those who take advice" (Proverbs 13:10). I am convinced that most quarrels and conflicts originate in our pride. Most of us think we are right most of the time. We believe we are smarter, wiser and that we know better than our spouses. We push our ideas and opinions. When they have another opinion, we are offended. We fight back. We argue. The Bible lays out a very specific challenge about pride: "Clothe yourselves with humility toward one another, because, 'God opposes the proud but gives grace to the humble'" (1 Peter 5:5). When we clothe ourselves with pride and arrogance, conflict and quarrels are inevitable. If, on the other hand, we realize that we don't know everything and that our spouses might just be right, we will find ourselves living in far greater harmony.

A Critical Spirit

Closely associated with pride is an attitude of criticism. It creeps into our marriages without our seeing it. Over the weeks, months and years we become critical of one another. We begin picking at each other and focusing on each other's faults. Our words and tones become more and more negative. "Drive out the mocker, and out goes strife; quarrels and insults are ended" (Proverbs 22:10). Quarrels and insults come from having a mocking or critical attitude. We need to examine our minds, hearts and words for this deadly, sinful habit.

Both husbands and wives can be guilty of having a critical spirit. I have seen many men use their position of leadership in marriage as an excuse to berate and downgrade their wives. A women married to a man like this looks beaten down, crushed and depressed. But I have also seen women who fulfill the words of the following passage all too well:

> A quarrelsome wife is like
> a constant dripping on a rainy day;
> restraining her is like restraining the wind
> or grasping oil with the hand
> (Proverbs 27:15-16).

Some women reason this way: *My husband is hearing only 10% of what I say, so here is what I'll do: I will increase what I say by a factor of 10, and he will hear 100% of what I want him to hear.*" This may sound like flawless logic, but it will only drive her husband further away!

Both husbands and wives must make every effort to get rid of a critical, complaining spirit, remembering from 1 Corinthians 13:5 that "[love] keeps no record of wrongs." Look for the good in your spouse and dwell on that, not on the negative qualities! Philippians 4:8 says it well:

> Finally, brothers, whatever is true, whatever is noble, whatever is right, whatever is pure, whatever is lovely, whatever is admirable—if anything is excellent or praiseworthy— think about such things.

A Defensive Posture

"He who loves a quarrel loves sin; he who builds a high gate invites destruction" (Proverbs 17:19). Some of us come off as if we are always "spoiling" for a fight. No matter what is said, we will take the other point of view. We are not open to hearing another idea. The moment our spouses begin to express themselves, we fire off absolute, contrary opinions that shut down further discussion. "He who answers before listening—that is his folly and his shame" (Proverbs 18:13).

The greater our defensiveness, the more we provoke antagonism, close down communication and provoke arguments. We need to tear down our "high gate" of defensiveness and replace it with the open door of receptivity.

Inflammatory Words

"A gentle answer turns away wrath, but a harsh word stirs up anger" (Proverbs 15:1). The words we use set the tone of our relationship. If you want to escalate an argument, then throw in some choice adjectives like "stupid," "dumb" or "idiot," or try something like "You never..." or "You always...." Such demeaning and absolute statements immediately provoke anger and resistance. They can provide the spark to a volatile situation that makes it explode. We need to remember that "reckless words pierce like a sword, but the tongue of the wise brings healing" (Proverbs 12:18). We also need to remember that when we are angry, we need to control our emotions and not use foolish words. "A fool gives full vent to his anger, but a wise man keeps himself under control" (Proverbs 29:11).

In looking back over my life and reviewing the times I have lost my temper, I cannot remember any good that came of it. I well remember, however, the harm and hurt that my angry words have caused some of my closest relationships. And I recall the times my reckless words have hurt the woman I love more than anyone else on earth. Let us resolve not to allow the words of anger and extremism to become a part of any conversation with our spouses.

Unresolved Issues and Feelings

Therefore each of you must put off falsehood and speak truthfully to his neighbor, for we are all members of one body. "In your anger do not sin": Do not let the sun go down while you are still angry, and do not give the devil a foothold (Ephesians 4:25-27).

As we said earlier, differences and conflicts will arise in the best of marriages. Even in a simple difference of opinion, we should openly talk and hash out our thoughts until we reach agreement. If we have hurt one another's feelings, we must openly discuss it and resolve it.

The passage above says that we must speak truthfully to each other. If we can let our opinions go or resolve our feelings without discussion, that is well and good. But if that opinion or feeling persists and is bothering us, we simply must get it out in the open and talk about it with our spouses. To do less is to be dishonest and allows attitudes of resentment to fester within us.

It is best to resolve conflicts and hurt feelings on the day they occur. This is what is meant by not letting the sun go down on our anger. Some of the most tragic situations I have ever seen in my counseling experience have come about because husbands and wives have held in hurt feelings for days, weeks, months or even years. Such unexpressed attitudes destroy happiness and corrode love. You cannot allow the love of false peace to keep you from seeking true harmony. It is better to have a difficult discussion than to brood. Believe me, these feelings will eventually come out under pressure, and it will not be a pretty sight!

Cure for Conflict

An offended brother is more unyielding
than a fortified city,
and disputes are like the barred gates of a citadel
(Proverbs 18:19).

For conflict to be resolved and cured, it must be talked out. There is no way around it. This means that in any marriage, both people must agree that if the other person wants to talk, they will cooperate. It cannot be that one partner shuts down, retreats, clams up and refuses to talk. Such behavior is foolish, selfish and destructive. It is also unfair. Whether your refusal to speak is out of fear or anger, or is a manipulative tool, you must realize that it will lead to ultimate disaster.

Having said that, please note that such discussions must occur at the proper time and place. Sometimes our timing is very unwise. We get into an intense discussion just before we get out of the car to meet friends for dinner; we have a heavy talk just as one of us is leaving for work; or we argue in front of other people. And worst of all, we quarrel within earshot of our children. Be mature enough to call for a discussion at the proper time—it can even be arranged in advance. Try saying something like this: "It is obvious we have a lot to talk about, and we need a time and place to have a discussion. When is the soonest time we can get some time to talk?" Most spouses will honor this approach. And when we function in this way, we are well on the way to resolving conflict quickly in our marriages. Having said all this, what are the specific cures for conflict?

Search for Truth

Be more concerned for *what* is right than *who* is right. In the midst of any disagreement, take a deep breath and ask yourself: *What is the truth*? As hard as it may be to do, forget about your position and your pride. Realize that the truth is the truth, no matter who believes it or how hard we argue against it. I am reminded of Paul's statement in 2 Corinthians 13:8, "For we cannot do anything against the truth, but only for the truth." It is foolish to continue to argue a position that is even partially wrong. Be big enough to step above the smoke and fire, see the facts of the situation and admit the truth to yourself and to your spouse.

Apologize

Apologize for anything you have said or done that is wrong. "Who can say, 'I have kept my heart pure; I am clean and without sin'"? (Proverbs 20:9). In most conflict situations, there is usually wrong on both people's parts. Ultimately, you are only responsible for what you have done wrong, and you can only change one person in the world—yourself. So, rather than trying to change your spouse, decide to change yourself first. Do not preoccupy yourself with whose wrongs are greater or smaller; take responsibility for your mistakes and admit them openly. Follow this simple procedure:

1) Apologize first. Don't wait for your spouse to come crawling to you. Instead, deal with yourself before God. Then go to him or her and admit what you have already confessed to God.

2) Apologize without excusing or minimizing. We can offer some pretty lame apologies which actually sound more like accusations: "If I have offended you, I am very sorry," or "I am sorry that I responded to your terrible, sinful outburst of temper by getting a little impatient in return." These kinds of statements are not true apologies or expressions of sorrow,

but are manipulative tools. If we learn to have godly sorrow for our wrongs before the Lord, we can easily apologize to our spouses without excusing or minimizing.

3) Apologize honestly. Do not quickly take blame out of fear or a love of false peace. If you were wrong, say so. If you were not, don't act as if you were.

4) Ask for forgiveness. Clearly express the words "Will you please forgive me?" to your spouse. So many times we are too proud to actually ask this all-important question.

Find Common Ground

Look for points of agreement. Often we become so focused on our points of difference that we do not realize we may, in fact, have large areas of agreement. Work from your points of unity to your areas of difference rather than the other way around, and you will be more successful in coming together for a solution.

Sharpen the Focus

We should clarify what exactly we are disagreeing about. Sometimes issues become clouded, facts fade into the background and emotions hold sway. "The purposes of a man's heart are deep waters, but a man of understanding draws them out" (Proverbs 20:5). If you take time to carefully and patiently listen to your spouse's point of view, you can understand what is specifically bothering him or her. Work together towards a solution.

No Side Issues

We can make things worse by bringing up other issues in the middle of a conflict. It is best to tackle one issue at a time and carry it to conclusion. If we resurrect past disagreements, we won't make progress. Also, if we hide what we are really feeling by focusing on a side issue, the conflict will not be resolved and much energy will be wasted.

Forgive Completely

"Bear with each other and forgive whatever grievances you may have against one another. Forgive as the Lord forgave you" (Colossians 3:13). The Bible speaks in very strong terms about the need for complete forgiveness. The longer I live, the more I am convinced that forgiving others is one of the most difficult challenges we face. Sometimes we want the other person to understand completely how much they have hurt us before we forgive them. This is wrong and simply does not happen. Others cannot fully understand all that we feel any more than we can understand all that God felt when he gave up Jesus on the cross to pay for our sins. Many of us have held our spouses' mistakes and shortcomings over their heads for far too long—it is time to completely forgive them as they have requested. And we must always remember that forgiveness is the right thing to do even when they have not requested it (Luke 23:34). We need to say the words "I forgive you" and release them from the bondage of our unforgiveness.

Work Through the Healing Process

If feelings have been deeply hurt, it may take some time for the wounds to completely heal. But the presence of continued hurt or difficulty does not necessarily mean there has not been forgiveness. It may simply mean that there needs to be a time devoted to mending the wounds.

If you have hurt your spouse, you must understand that healing is a process. You can help by giving reassurances of your continued sorrow even after the discussion is over. Later on that day, or the next day, or the day after, you need to say again the words "I want you know that I am very sorry, and I will do everything I can to not let it happen again." Give continual assurances of your love, devotion and affection after times of reconciliation. All of these special words and increased attention will enable your spouse to grow out of, and through, the time of pain to the time of healing.

Get Help!

"He who listens to a life-giving rebuke will be at home among the wise" (Proverbs 15:31). There are times when, in spite of our best efforts, we cannot resolve our conflicts ourselves. We need outside help. This is when we should call in responsible Christian friends or experienced church leaders to help. Paul suggests this in Philippians 4:2-3 when he appeals to two quarreling women to agree and then asks one of his coworkers to assist them in coming to peace. It brings no shame upon us that we sometimes need the help of mature friends to assist us in resolving conflict. Some of us are too proud to admit our need. We want to keep our problems to ourselves. Certainly, we should first make every effort to solve things alone, but there comes a time when we must reach out for assistance. The goal of this kind of mediation is to get us to the point that we not only resolve this conflict, but that we learn how to better resolve any future disagreements that may arise.

Unity in marriage is a precious thing. It is our conviction that the principles presented in this chapter will help you to learn how to have a more peaceful marriage and to quickly and effectively restore the peace when it has been lost.

CHAPTER 10

In the Long Run

"Therefore what God has joined
together, let man not separate."

MATTHEW 19:6

Consider these two vital questions: First, will your marriage make it to the end? Second, will you make it to the end as better people and with a better marriage than when you began?

The headlines are full of marriages that began with high promise and ended in disaster. From the storybook marriages of royalty to the glamour of Hollywood to the neighbors next-door, more couples are not making it to the finish.

God intends marriage to last a lifetime. His goal is for us to hit the finish in better shape than when we began, so this should also be our goal. Forging a relationship that joyfully makes it to the end will be one of our greatest achievements in life, and will take the best we have to give.

How can we go about building a marriage that makes it in the long run?

Make Your Marriage a Top Priority

You must continually place your marriage in a position of crucial priority. We have said throughout this book that your relationship to your spouse is your most important human bond. Relationships are dynamic; they do not stay in place without continual rededication and renewal. If we commit ourselves to building a relationship and then back away, the relationship dies. No long-lasting marriage happens by accident. It lasts because both partners keep it as a top priority in their hearts.

Many marriages die because they are taken for granted. Husbands and wives assume that the love and dedication that was invested in the past is sufficient to carry them through. Not so! Commitment to each other must be continually renewed, just as commitment to Jesus is renewed by taking up our crosses daily (Luke 9:23).

Renewing involves doing those things that nourish your relationship and assure your spouse of your continuing love. It means a continuing commitment to communication. It means not allowing other activities or people to displace your spouse from the place of primary love. It means devoting yourself to a private, intimate friendship on a daily basis, and it means cultivating your relationship by going away alone for special times together. These and many other efforts will have to be made to keep the fires burning.

In the book of Revelation, Jesus chides the church in Ephesus for losing her first love (Revelation 2:4). Have you lost your first love for your spouse? Have you lost the excitement, joy and wonder of your early days? Where is the heady anticipation and mystery that was yours on your wedding day? Does your heart beat faster when you see each other across a room anymore? Do you still give those special knowing looks that say you care? Some regard the loss of these feelings as inevitable with the passing of time. They call it "maturity." Jesus calls it a loss of first love. His solution? He called upon them to remember the height from which they had fallen. He urged them to repent (change their attitude) and do the things they did at first. He challenged them to listen, to take him seriously and to do whatever it took to regain their original feelings (Revelation 2:5-7). In short, they had lost their first love because they had ceased to put Jesus as top priority in their lives. If your marriage is to endure in the long run, you must always make it the supreme human relationship in your life.

Draw Close Through Trials

A man of many companions may come to ruin,
    but there is a friend who sticks closer than a brother
(Proverbs 18:24).

Draw closer to each other as you face life's trials. These challenges will either drive you apart or bring you together. That trials come is inevitable, and they will come in many forms: the loss of a job, financial strain, difficulty with relatives, pregnancy, childbirth, child rearing, sexual difficulties, differences of opinion, illness, the death of loved ones, etc. How you respond to trials determines whether your marriage dies or flourishes.

God allows trials to come into our lives to develop our character and make us more dependent upon him. (See Romans 5:3-4 and James 1:2-4.) In the same way, are meant to draw us nearer to others and to our spouses.

> Two are better than one,
>> because they have a good return for their work:
> If one falls down,
>> his friend can help him up.
> But pity the man who falls
>> and has no one to help him up!
> Also, if two lie down together, they will keep warm.
>> But how can one keep warm alone?
> Though one may be overpowered,
>> two can defend themselves.
> A cord of three strands is not quickly broken
> (Ecclesiastes 4:9-12).

When we undergo difficulties, we especially feel the need for friends, and what closer friends do we have than our spouses? Trials should draw you closer in marital friendship. If trials cause you to withdraw from your spouse, then somehow you have responded wrongly.

Geri and I were deeply in love in the early years of our marriage, but now we love each other more and are closer than before. Why is this so? It is partly due to the passage of time and our individual growth, but the greater reason is that we have gone through so much together. Our love has been seasoned by staying beside each other in trying and difficult times. We have stood together through the death of loved ones, financial strain, the illnesses of our children, persecution for our faith, and difficulties with friends and family. We have seen each other at our worst and at our best. This has produced in both of our hearts a greater compassion and appreciation for each other. In addition, each of us has contributed to the other's happiness, strength and character development in these trials. We know that there were times when we could not have gone on without each other, and we love each other all the more for it.

The tapestries of our marriages will have in them threads of many colors—bright colors for days of happiness and darker ones for days of trial. All of the threads are woven by God into a beautiful pattern that is our life story. The longer we stay together, the more we will be able to look back, see God's plan and feel a deepening gratitude that we have stayed together through it all.

Deepen in Spirituality

"Though one may be overpowered, two can defend themselves. A cord of three strands is not quickly broken" (Ecclesiastes 2:12). Applied to marriage, the two strands represent husband and wife, and the third strand is their common relationship with God. God and his love are the binding that holds a marriage together and provides a deepening love through the years. Paul appealed to the Philippians to be united for the sake of Jesus Christ (Philippians 2:1-4), and he said in Colossians 1:17 that "in him [Christ] all things hold together." It is *in Christ* that a marriage holds together and stays strong. The power of our own unaided love is not enough because weakness and selfishness undermine it, but the love of God never fails.

It is imperative that we continue to grow in our individual walks with God as time passes. The call for disciples to grow in maturity is given repeatedly in the Scriptures (Philippians 3:12-16; 2 Corinthians 3:18; 1 Thessalonians 4:10; Hebrews 6:1-2; 2 Peter 3:18). If we grow personally closer to God, we will draw closer to one another. Couples who allow their faith to diminish and their love for God to wane through the years end up losing their love for one another. Couples who together grow stronger in faith and who remain firm in commitment to God have a deepening love for each other. As we see God answer our prayers, our gratitude grows. As we turn to God when we have failed him and each other, our humility increases, and our love is renewed. As we see God's blessing resting upon our children as we raise them to follow Jesus, our sense of accomplishment and fulfillment is unparalleled. All of this works to bind us together with unbreakable bonds.

Cultivate Quality Friendships

> Perfume and incense bring joy to the heart,
>   and the pleasantness of one's friend springs from
>   his earnest counsel
> (Proverbs 27:9).

Even couples with strong marriages need friends. We need other married couples to be our encouragers, our mentors and our faithful companions. We cannot make it to the end depending solely upon each other. There may be times when, as a couple, you have differences between the two of you that friends will have to step in and help you resolve. There will also be times when both of you are spiritually weak and you need the help of other friends to see you through.

Notice carefully: We need *quality* friends. By this, I mean people who will tell us what we need to hear, not what we want to hear. "Wounds from a friend can be trusted, but an enemy multiplies kisses" (Proverbs 27:6). True friends love us enough to tell us the truth even if it makes us uncomfortable or angry. Many people have friends who pat them on the back and cheer them up, but take it no further. We should therefore cultivate friendships with people who are strong, who speak their minds and who have the mind of Christ (1 Corinthians 2:16).

Our friends must be involved in our *real lives.* This means that we allow them into our lives on more than a superficial level. I am sure you know couples who are happy to have your friendship until you begin to probe beneath the surface. For example, if they are angry with each other, and you try to talk to them about it, they close ranks. They foolishly defend each other. Such people do not want genuine friends—they just want buddies. They want to have fun and enjoy some good times, but when conversation begins to get deep, they back off. Such couples are unable to sustain long-term relationships with other marrieds and will end up with chronic spiritual and marital problems because they will not listen to the people who care the most for them.

Let me ask you some important questions: How many other married people have you allowed into your real life? What other married friends of yours know the real scoop on the two of you? With how many couples have you had strong words, difficult confrontations, angry feelings and tearful conversations and have continued being friends? If you have broken away from people after these kinds of talks, then you have stepped away from one of the most valuable assets in helping you to have a long-lasting marriage—mature, quality friends.

Allow me to ask more questions: If you have these kinds of relationships, *how many* do you have? Do any of these people live in close proximity to you now? Are they consistently involved in your life? You may feel that you have this level of friendship, but the other couples that you are thinking of may not feel the same way about you. Perhaps you need to ask them if they feel free to bring up uncomfortable subjects with you. If there is hesitation, then you need to make it clear that you want them in your real life.

I remember one couple Geri and I worked to be close to for more than five years. We opened up our hearts to them and revealed to them our weaknesses and struggles. We tried to earn their trust with our own transparency, but they did not respond in kind. They would sometimes let on that they were unhappy with each other and in their marriage, but these admissions were always done guardedly. Finally, the husband opened up with me and told me how concerned he was about some issues in his wife's life. He had tried to talk to her for years about these problems but had made no progress. We agreed we would speak to her together.

The day came for our planned conversation, and we began talking. She got upset at some of the issues I brought up. He looked at me with a shocked expression, acted surprised, quickly backed away and came to her support. The session ended in disaster. At first, I couldn't believe what happened. Upon reflection, however, I realized this is what both of them had always done. They would criticize one another, but the minute Geri and I would try to help, they withdrew, especially when it came down to discussing it in front of us. I saw this man recently after an absence of years. It was obvious that things in the marriage were the same, that they were pretty much living separate lives. It was not difficult to see that he was still unhappy with her, and she with him. I was saddened but realized that we had done all we could and that they had made their choice, not only with us, but with many others who had longed for their friendship through the years.

Don't let this sad story become yours! Cultivate relationships with spiritual people—people of character—and let them into your real life.

Come to Terms with
Your Past and Your Weaknesses

> Therefore, since we are surrounded by such a great cloud of witnesses, let us throw off everything that hinders and the sin that so easily entangles, and let us run with perseverance the race marked out for us (Hebrews 12:1).

Our past may be our present. Problems from our childhood and upbringing that we have not recognized or resolved can destroy our marriage. Issues such as sexual and physical abuse, alcoholism, difficult or traumatic experiences, and the like, if left in our hearts unattended, can destroy our ability to trust our spouses and be close to them. Deal with the problems by discussing them with qualified Christian advisors. Get them out into the open with your spouse. Do not let your past destroy your future.

Unresolved events in the history of the marriage can also work as a destructive, corrosive influence. What am I talking about? Let me list a few examples: premarital sexual indiscretion with one another; unresolved arguments and hurtful words; differences over in-laws; disagreements in parenting; financial issues; ongoing sexual conflict—all kinds of things, even if they occurred many years past, can live on in our hearts to numb, deaden and destroy our love for each other. We simply must get these things out in the open, deal with them and leave them forgiven and resolved forever.

All of us have personal weaknesses. Hopefully, as disciples of Jesus, we recognize them and are striving to overcome them. If you do not know what they are, believe me, your spouse does! Some of us are oblivious to our weaknesses, or we minimize them. The sad truth is that our spouses must live with the real "us" and our real problems—even the ones we pretend we don't have!

We must come to terms with our besetting sins and depend on God to help us overcome them on a daily basis. The great flaw of Saul the Pharisee was his pride and self-righteousness. He was deeply broken and convicted of his sin when he became a disciple, and yet we know that even as Paul the apostle he still struggled with his pride many years later (2 Corinthians 12:7-10).

The apostle Peter compromised his convictions as he denied Jesus in the courtyard of the high priest. He made a similar mistake years later even as a mature, seasoned disciple when he backed down under pressure and would not fellowship the Gentile believers in Galatia (Galatians 2:11-14).

If men of this spiritual stature had ongoing character weaknesses, so will we! We must be deeply humble and continually depend on God to overcome them. A partner who does not face up to his or her character weaknesses hurts the long-term happiness of the marriage. There is simply no way to have a harmonious marriage when one or both of us have weaknesses that we will not face and change. We need to ask ourselves and our spouses this question: "Is there anything in my life that I need to face up to, that I am refusing to deal with, or dealing with reluctantly?" No matter how difficult it is to hear the answer, listen. Preserving our pride is not worth the price of ongoing conflict and tension in our marriage.

Fan the Flames

"Let him kiss me with the kisses of his mouth—
for your love is more delightful than wine"
(Song of Songs 1:2).

Since romantic love is like wine, it should get better with time! An ongoing great sex life is one of the keys to a marriage that prospers through the years.

One of the reasons we fear old age is that we are afraid of losing our physical attractiveness and our sexual powers. Who says that sex, sexuality and sexual excitement have to diminish as we get older? Where and by whom was this decreed? It may be true for some, but not for all. Sexual frequency may diminish as we get older (for some, this will be a welcome relief!) but that does not mean lessened desire, enjoyment or intensity.

Sex and romance should become more exciting as we get older. Why? Because of increased closeness—as our friendship gets better, the sex gets better. The longer a couple is together, the more they love each other and understand how to please each other. None of us should lose the joys of sex as we get older. Instead, we should work to cultivate an intensifying, increasing joy and pleasure as they years go by.

There may be some marriages in which the sexual experience legitimately decreases. This may happen due to illness or incapacitation. If this occurs, then our loyalty to each other will cause us to find other ways to draw close, even though our sexual life may be changed or diminished. But what must remain is a deep commitment to each other and a continuing sense of romance in our marriage, even with the absence of usual sexual intercourse. Couples that go through a temporary or permanent loss of ability of the usual ways of making love should still retain their deep attraction and commitment to each other. And even if your spouse is physically unable to perform as they once did, this is never an excuse for deserting them or losing your love for them.

Find and Use Your Talents

> For by the grace given me I say to every one of you: Do not think of yourself more highly than you ought, but rather think of yourself with sober judgment, in accordance with the measure of faith God has given you.... We have different gifts, according to the grace given us" (Romans 12:3, 6).

God has blessed each one of us with unique talents, and he grants us the opportunity and challenge to use them to his glory. It is vital that we all have a sober estimate of what our abilities and talents are and that we find a place in life to make our unique contributions. It is important for each person in a marriage to feel that individually and collectively they are being used in a way that makes a difference. If one or both of us feel that our lives count for little in God's scheme of things, there will be frustration which will spill over and cause problems in our marriage.

Each spouse should look out for the other by helping him or her to find a great niche in which to serve and function within God's kingdom. Husbands, if you feel like your wife is empty, bored and not feeling useful, then you need to be the one to help her to recognize her talents and find a place where she can use them. And wives, you need to do the same for your husbands.

God's kingdom is replete with opportunities for men and women to serve. In my years of ministry I have seen people who were overlooked by the world and who thought they had no talent literally come alive with joy and energy as their abilities were discovered and put to use in serving God and his church.

We can make mistakes coming and going. Some of us overestimate ourselves and think we have talent in areas that we do not. We need help in figuring this out, or it will lead to frustration and conflict. On the other hand, others of us underestimate ourselves—we have talent and ability that has never been developed. This is where a wise, loving spouse can help us. Mature, spiritual friends can also come to our assistance. Find out what your talents are, and use them to God's glory! Do not allow your life to continue on with a sense of failure, lost opportunity and unused potential. It will hurt you, it will hurt God's kingdom, and it will hurt your marriage as well. Find your place of highest usefulness, and go to work!

We opened this chapter by asking the question "Will your marriage make it to the end?" and "Will you make it to the end as better people and with better marriages than when you began?" The answers to these questions touch upon some of the most important issues of our lives. The good news is that none of us is stuck where we are! Even if we feel we have wasted valuable years, we are only a decision away from turning things around. So let's get on with the business of living! God says,

> Forget the former things;
>   do not dwell on the past.
> See, I am doing a new thing!
>   Now it springs up; do you not perceive it?
> I am making a way in the desert
>   and streams in the wasteland
> (Isaiah 43:18-19).

CHAPTER 11

Up from Defeat

I will make rivers flow on barren heights,
and springs within the valleys.
I will turn the desert into pools of water,
and the parched ground into springs.

ISAIAH 41:18

We have said much, but we have not yet said everything. We wanted to close this book by giving you some hope that your marriage can be different. Here are some real-life situations that we have seen turn from disaster and defeat to success and victory. The names have been changed, but the people are real. These examples are drawn from the marriages we have worked with over a twenty-five-year period of ministry. Our faith has been strengthened beyond measure by seeing the power of God work to bring love and joy out of some of the most miserable and defeated situations imaginable.

John and Michelle
Life Wears You Down

When we came to know John and Michelle, they both had a vacant, dead look in their eyes. They were discouraged, depressed and weary. It seemed they had everything to be happy about: healthy children, a beautiful home and a solid position in the full-time ministry. But things were not going so well. John was discouraged because of a sense of failure in his work and the recent loss of his beloved father. He felt ineffective in leading others because he knew that he was not close to his wife and was failing in leading his own family. He was well-educated and intelligent but did not know how to express his hopes, dreams, needs and hurts to those he loved, including his wife. His primary manner of reaching out to his wife was through his longings for sexual affection. He felt unsupported, unloved and alone in the midst of his pain. He was dying slowly from within.

Michelle, though possessing a positive and outgoing personality, was unhappy with herself, her marriage and her children. Part of the reason for her sexual unresponsiveness was that she knew she was many pounds overweight (as was John). This embarrassed her and made her sexually indifferent. And, despite being a warm person, she lacked the sensitivity to understand John's difficulties and feelings of failure.

Talking to John and Michelle separately and then comparing notes later was quite an experience. They were poles apart in recounting the simplest situations involving the two of them. For a while we were mystified, but later we realized this was a key to solving their problems. Both of them were so completely self-focused that they could not begin to comprehend the other's point of view. They could learn to resolve conflict only if they began to make serious efforts to understand and empathize with each other.

What did it take to change? John and Michelle had to face up to their individual deficiencies. Both had to see the mistakes that had gotten them where they were, own up to them and decide to change. They needed to speak openly to each other about their frustrations and disappointments in the relationship and to be willing to hear the other person's point of view. And both had to decide to recommit themselves to their marriage and to get their spiritual and physical lives in order.

Today John and Michelle are happily in love and, have made great strides in overcoming the mistakes and defeats of their past. Their communication has radically improved, as has their romantic life. All of this has taken much work, patience and self-examination, but they are now much more aware of what they need to do to meet one another's needs.

Dan and Joanna
The Death of a Child

Dan and Joanna never dreamed it would happen to them. They came home one afternoon and saw the emergency vehicles and a crowd of neighbors gathered in the parking lot outside their apartment. The devastating news came crashing in upon them—their infant child left earlier with a baby-sitter, had just died, a victim of Sudden Infant Death Syndrome. Once they overcame the initial shock, terrible problems set in. Dan and Joanna began resorting to drugs and alcohol to deaden the pain of their grief. They became increasingly distant from one another and both ended up committing adultery. Dan had multiple affairs, even with some of Joanna's closest friends. They had a semblance of normal life as jobs, school and the daily routine continued, but the pallor of death hung over them. Each evening, they would drink themselves to numbness, and eventually Dan began to acquire and abuse prescription drugs.

But then Dan and Joanna became disciples of Jesus Christ, and that has radically changed their lives. They have faced up to their drug addiction and have been completely open with each other concerning their adultery. They are now free of any drug use and have experienced a joyous renewal of their love. The sadness over the loss of their infant son remains, but instead of despair, they have confidence that they will one day be reunited with him in heaven! And they have hope that they will influence their other children to follow Christ.

Norm and Kristin
Talent and Success Are Not Enough

They were the classic story: young, good-looking, thirty-something, two beautiful children, making good money. But it all fell apart. They had both become disciples of Jesus in their college years, but in time, had become spiritually dead. Norm's sexual lust lead him into an increasing addiction to pornography, masturbation and eventually, into a homosexual affair. He knew what he was doing was wrong and would never have believed he would fall so far, but he felt irresistibly drawn down a terrible path. He tried counseling and therapy groups, but to no avail. He later related that he felt completely enslaved and did not know how he could ever change.

Kristin was uninvolved in her husband's real life. In her intense need to prove herself, she became preoccupied with other people, causes and concerns to the neglect of her marriage. Their sexual relationship diminished and almost disappeared. Above all, she was neither close to her husband emotionally nor there for him to help him overcome his struggles. Norm lied to Kristin about what he was doing, and she was too afraid to act on her intuition that there could be deeper, darker issues in his life.

Norm decided to face up to what he had done and seek spiritual guidance in overcoming his problems. Working with their advisors, Norm and Kristin decided it would be best for Norm to move out of his home for a period of days to sort out his feelings and to decide the direction he wanted to go. Though she was angry and heartbroken over what Norm had done, Kristin had to face up to her weaknesses as well. She and the children hurt over Norm's absence but accepted that it was for the best and prayed that he would do the right thing. After a protracted period of soul-searching, Norm made the decision to come back to God and to get the help he needed to be a faithful husband and father. He began to visit with his family on a regular basis and finally, with counseling and teaching, Norm and Kristin reached the point that they were ready to live together again. They made a rededication of their lives to God and to each other in a public renewal of their wedding vows.

Today they are happily married, and if you were to meet them, you would not know that they had been through such a horrible ordeal. Norm wrestles occasionally with sexual temptation and even with homosexual thoughts, but he and Kristin have an exciting, happy sex life and he is able to be honest with her about his struggles. They are a shining example of how the power of God and the working of the body of Christ can bring people through unspeakable defeat to a place of victory and hope for the future.

Carl and Dana
Anger and Deceit

Carl had always struggled with anger and bitterness. It seemed to be second nature to him and had been reinforced from his youngest years by the difficult experience of being raised by a negligent, alcoholic father. Dana, too, had lived a hard life and had seen the worst that the world could do. She developed a stubborn, deceitful character as a result. After they became disciples, their lives changed in many ways, but the marriage relationship remained a continual source of difficulty. He was harsh, she was disrespectful, and they seemed to argue constantly.

Dana appeared to be easygoing, but inside was fearful of Carl's anger. She had been honest with him about some things in her past but only to a point. She had deceived him about an affair which she had, fearing that if the truth ever came out, it would destroy what little love Carl had left for her. Reasoning that his critical and negative nature simply could not overcome another disappointment, she withheld the truth.

Deception always leads to distance in a relationship. Although in the dark about the facts, Carl was perceptive enough to sense that something was amiss. His criticalness and anger intensified. With every harsh word and scowling look she received, Dana felt more confirmed in her belief that she needed to keep up the lie to preserve her marriage.

Finally, she decided she could not continue her charade. Dana sought the counsel of friends, who urged her to tell Carl the truth. She mustered up her courage and her faith and did so. He reacted with anger and resentment at first, but ultimately decided he must forgive her.

Looking back, Dana is immensely relieved to have gotten rid of this terrible burden. She now finds that she is able to trust herself and her husband completely. And in spite of his past harshness, she is able to love Carl in a way she never has before. For his part, Carl is now confident that Dana has been completely truthful with him. His suspicions are finally laid to rest. He struggles with anger and bitterness from time to time when he recalls her lies and her affair, but now he knows what he is dealing with, as does she. Carl and Dana have discovered the power of truth and grace and they now have a new life together.

Allen and Theresa
Problems with In-Laws

Allen and Theresa loved each other very much, but there was a problem—both sets of in-laws were unhappy with their marriage.

Allen's parents never fully accepted Theresa. They were well-to-do socialites, but Theresa was from a blue-collar, religiously conservative background. They felt she was unworthy of their son, and they told him this in no uncertain terms. Allen finally revealed his parents' attitudes to Theresa, which only confirmed the aloofness she had felt from them for years. Worse still, she detected a subtle change in Allen's demeanor when his parents were on the scene. She discussed her perceptions with Allen, but he minimized her feelings and tried to persuade her that he was not influenced by his parents' attitudes. She became bitter and resentful. She clashed with her in-laws on a number of issues. She came across as a self-righteous critic rather than a loving and concerned daughter-in-law. They reacted with anger and withdrawal and the relationship deteriorated.

Allen considered Theresa's parents' religion to be laughably naive. He regarded the negativity and legalism of their faith with disdain and wondered why anyone would believe in something that caused them such misery. The memory of how Theresa compromised her morals to become sexually involved with him before their marriage caused Allen to lose even more respect for her and her beliefs. He ridiculed her parents' faith to their face. They were deeply hurt and withdrew in silence. Theresa was angry that her husband spoke so cruelly and insensitively to her parents, even though she agreed largely with his assessment of their spiritual condition. When Allen and Theresa moved away from her family to another part of the country, her bitterness increased even more. Allen's involvement in his new career position, Theresa's longing for her family and continued conflicts with the in-laws escalated tensions to the breaking point.

Finally, Allen and Theresa came to a dynamic church that was Bible-based and positive in its message. Allen, with the attitude "you will never convince me," sat down to study the Bible with the church leaders and ended up as a believer! He soon made the decision to be a disciple and was baptized into Christ. Theresa realized that her past religion had been one of legalism and duty, and not the life of love and joy that Jesus promised. She joined Allen in becoming a true disciple of Jesus.

Allen and Theresa have asked each other for forgiveness for the hurt they caused each other and have done their best to make amends with their parents. The relationship with the in-laws is still not strong, but Allen and Theresa are hopeful. What has changed the most is Allen and Theresa's marriage. They are now joyfully in love with each other and are thrilled with their new-found faith. Their hope and prayer is that their parents will recognize the changes in them, will forgive them for the mistakes they have made, and will one day share with them in the new spiritual life they have found.

Ed and Anna
Fix It Yourselves

When Ed and Anna came into our ministry from another city, they had a reputation for having serious marriage problems. They had been counseled for years by some of the best, but they never seemed to change. And that was the problem—they weren't learning from what they had been taught.

The specific weakness in their marriage was found in their failure to fulfill their proper roles. Ed tended to be unloving, insensitive and harsh. He had a background of sexual abuse and had lost his father at an early age. This forced him to grow up quickly in order to help his mother run the family. All of this produced in him strength and forcefulness, but left him with a diminished ability to give and receive love. His wife often felt neglected and was starving for attention and affection.

In spite of her sensitivity, Anna was strong-willed and proud. She was disrespectful to Ed and tended to want to run the show. When her feelings were hurt, she became self-pitying and defensive. It was virtually impossible for Ed to challenge her. Whenever he did, she would begin to cry and feel sorry for herself even as she fended him off. Her supersensitivity and her stubbornness made life difficult for them both.

As we worked with them, they would continually bring up each other's past mistakes. They were classic users of "always" and "never" and were experts at dissecting each other's character flaws. After talks with us, their relationship would improve, but they would come back in a few days or weeks with a new problem. In reality, the problem was not new—it was simply a different version of the same old pattern.

We decided that this had gone on long enough. We told Ed and Anna that they were using our advice as a crutch. We stated that it was high time that they began to face up to their character weaknesses and make long-overdue changes in their lives and marriage dynamics. We informed them that no more would we give them a periodic "marriage fix"—from now on, we expected them to fix themselves. When they had a conflict, they were to sit down together, and with God's help, humbly work it out. We assured them that we would be there for them, but that we would not live their lives for them.

Ed and Anna looked at us with stunned disbelief. This seemed too shockingly simple. Didn't they need continual counseling and discipling to help them solve their problems? Didn't being a disciple mean that you got advice? We explained to them that the purpose of discipling and counseling is to bring people to the point of maturity so that they can begin to conquer problems rather than be continually overcome by them. It was now time for them to make a decision to grow up. We told them that when the next conflict arose, we would expect the two of them to work it out. They left our talk shaken, but determined to follow through.

Ed and Anna made remarkable progress. They still had to wrestle with their old character weaknesses, but they learned to apologize for their mistakes and help each other get through the problems. They experienced the victory of being able to patiently express what bothers or angers them and to resolve their differences and feelings. They gained greater confidence and became more fun to be with as well! Like every married couple, they continued to need help from time to time, but, with God's help, they achieved greater and greater success in resolving their own conflicts.

⸻

We recount these stories with the purpose of giving hope. We tell them so that all of us can see that no matter how bad things may be, there is a way out. We began this book with a statement of three convictions, and we want to end with them as well:

•Any two people can change.
•Any marriage can be fixed.
•Any marriage can become great.

The power and love of God are available for you. We are not saying it will be easy. We are not promising that your spouse will necessarily do what he or she should do. We are saying that the decisions you must make are up to you and should be made as soon as possible. Let the changes begin with you! And when both of you are willing to give your lives to God and to each other, there is no defeat that cannot be turned into a victory !

One More Thought...

We have just spent four chapters discussing "Reality." One of the greatest realities is that life is often hard! Simple as this may sound, it is a fact of life that many of us need not only to accept, but embrace. I fought this for a long time, and I believe that many of you are fighting it as well. During those early years I would deal with every obstacle or difficulty I encountered as if it were the last hurdle to get over before I would finally experience permanent happiness and contentment. Peace and enjoyment always seemed to be "just around the corner" or "over the next hill." But I found that every time one problem was resolved, a new problem was already heading my way, once again postponing my peace and happiness.

Why am I writing these things in a book on marriage? Because these are the things that weigh heavily on our lives and affect all of our closest relationships. These are the realities that few of us had experienced or understood when we started out as newlyweds. After numerous letdowns and disappointments, I finally had to face the fact that life would always have its challenges and difficulties and that those very ups and downs would be the tools God would use to make me strong and righteous.

The storms of adversity will come into all of our lives— some minor, others devastating. We will go through financial challenges, job difficulties, in-law problems, the exhaustion of raising small children, and the challenges of raising teenagers. But then the storms will come that completely rock our worlds and break our hearts—the storms of sickness, death, loss and loneliness.

The strain and stress of such situations pull at a marriage and expose its weaknesses. Instead of allowing the challenges to pull you apart, you must learn to face them head-on, and to face them *together.* Sadly, many couples never learn this lesson, and so their marriages do not survive the stress of serious difficulty. Husbands and wives must hold on to each other at these times. They must fight through the temptation to blow up in anger and despair, to blame the other person or to withdraw emotionally.

Support each other. Understand that you may react and respond very differently to pain and hurt. Learn to extend love and comfort, even when you are deeply hurting yourself. Turn to God together. When all is said and done, these bitter-sweet moments may become some of the most treasured memories in your life together. You may never be the same after storms pass, but you can be better people with a stronger marriage.

While there is nothing we can do to prevent challenging, and even devastating, things from happening, the one thing we can (and must) control is our response to them. Sam always says, "It is not what happens *to* you, but what happens *in* you that counts." It is so easy to allow problems to dominate our thinking and steal our joy. Instead of seeing the blessings and the good in our lives, we focus on the bad things. We become embittered, resentful, negative and cynical. How many of us have known people who were positive and pleasant in their younger years, but who became critical and negative as they grew older? None of us will have a trouble-free existence, but the Bible commands us to rejoice always (Philippians 4:4). True happiness is a product of who we are on the inside. We can decide to be grateful, righteous and joyful no matter what our circumstances may be.

If we maintain a positive, upbeat spirit during hard times, then God will be able to use them as he intended—to refine us:

> Not only so, but we also rejoice in our sufferings, because we know that suffering produces perseverance; perseverance, character; and character, hope. And hope does not disappoint us... (Romans 5:3-5).

Adversities can teach us compassion and patience as nothing else can. There is much about life we cannot fully understand until we have experienced its hurts and difficulties. Trials have a way of putting our view of the world and of ourselves into perspective, exposing what is important and true, and what is not. Hardships can make the weak person stronger and tougher, and the strong person softer and more sensitive. They can humble us and bring us low and yet also give us a godly greatness.

Someone once said, "Life is hard and then we die." That is not the whole story, but real life does have its problems and its difficulties. However, we must not allow the challenges to rob us of happiness and to destroy our marriages. Remember the vows you made to one another: "In sickness and in health, for richer or for poorer, for better or for worse, 'til death do us part." You made the commitment to stick with each other, and with God, to the end. Let the hard times drive you closer to God and closer to one another. Go through the bad times, but dwell on all that is positive and good. In the words of the apostle Paul,

> Whatever is true, whatever is noble, whatever is right, whatever is pure, whatever is lovely, whatever is admirable— if anything is excellent or praiseworthy—think about such things (Philippians 4:8).

Learn to see the healing through the pain, the laughter through the tears, and the victories through the defeats; and when you come to the end, you will be standing tall and strong—together.

Geri Laing

Epilogue

In writing *Friends and Lovers* we have tried to deal with a number of very specific issues ranging from communication to finances to the sexual relationship. Read the different chapters of this book over and over again as needed. As you apply the things we have addressed, I sincerely hope you will see great changes begin to take place in your marriage.

However, as you near the end of this book, you may be feeling quite overwhelmed. There may be so many things that you (and your spouse) need to change that you hardly know where to begin! Most of us do better when we can simplify and condense the myriad of concepts we have learned into one or two basic principles that will apply in every situation. I believe there is one such principle that, when applied to marriage, will simplify—if not completely solve—almost every problem.

When I married at the age of twenty-one, very few of my closest friends were yet married. Aside from a few great examples to follow, I had only my Bible, God's instruction book on life, to teach me how to be a great wife. There was one scripture I held on to during those early years of marriage and still rely upon as the great principle and promise of the Christian life: "If anyone would come after me, he must deny himself and take up his cross daily and follow me. *For whoever wants to save his live will lose it, but whoever loses his life for me will save it*" (Luke 9:23-24, emphasis mine).

For many of us, our marriage problems are no more complicated than our own deep selfishness. We want what we want and will gripe, complain, push and mope until we get it. We are nothing more than grown-up children, bickering and fighting to get what we want. Such selfishness affects every part of our married lives, from the way we talk to one another in the kitchen to the way we make love in the bedroom. It determines how we spend our time and how we spend (or don't spend) our money. I realize there may be other complicated issues that need to be addressed, but if you would start here, by recognizing and dealing with your *own* selfishness (not your spouse's), your marriage would be incredibly different! Better yet, if *both* of you would make a decision to consider each other's feelings more than you do your own, I can assure you that the changes in your life together would be immediate, dramatic and more fulfilling than you can possibly imagine.

Bottom line, marriage is all about selflessness. It is being willing to put your own self aside for the good of another person. Luke 9:24 is the great paradox of life: Lose your life and you will find it. Long-term fulfillment will never come without unselfish sacrifice. This is a fact of life and is a bedrock principle of marriage.

Certainly there are some dysfunctional situations in which one person allows himself or herself to be abused by another person in cruel and ungodly ways. In those situations there comes a time when the abused spouse must become stronger and tougher and must take some difficult stands; however, this is not where most couples are. While there are some marriages that fail because of violence and abuse, far more marriages end or die because husbands and wives are just too selfish to really care about someone else more than, *or even as much as,* they care about themselves. How different most of our marriages would be if we began to genuinely think about our spouses and their needs instead of just our own!

I am reminded of what I learned as "The Golden Rule" when I was a child: "Do unto others as you would have them do unto you." This little rule was almost magical in its results when applied to friendships and childhood relationships. What if we put this simple rule into practice in our marriages? How do you want to be treated by your spouse? How would you like him or her to speak to you? What is the tone of voice you would like him or her to use? What are the compliments and comments you would like to hear? What are the thoughtful things that would say to you, "I love you"? Turn it around and do for him or her as you would like it done for you. Try it for a day or for a week. Better yet, make unselfishness the practice of your life. For many of us this will be the beginning of amazing changes!

In closing, let us be reminded that God's plan has always been that marriage should be a relationship of love and companionship that spans a lifetime. It is definitely not his plan that it become empty or dull as the years pass, or that it become a battleground where wars are fought with harsh words, icy withdrawals and bitter resentment.

Have you ever been around a couple who have been together for a long, long time and still care deeply for one another? Nothing is quite so moving or so desirable. They wear an air of comfortability and contentment. A quiet understanding passes between them. They sometimes seem to communicate without words, and when they do speak, one can finish a sentence that the other starts. Even their appearances begin to be the same. Is it just the fact that they both now have gray hair and wear glasses, or is it that they have been around each other for so long that they have taken on some of the same facial expressions? No one can say, but the fact remains that over the course of many years two lives have truly blended into one. What a great accomplishment! A successful, loving marriage that does not just *exist*, but *thrives*. A relationship built solidly over the years with the building blocks of shared laughter and tears, good times and hard times, victories and defeats. Friends and lovers…forever!

Geri Laing

Courtship, Dating and Engagement

A wife of noble character who can find?

PROVERBS 31:10

This is a book about marriage, but I am sure some of you singles are reading it with high hopes for the future! I wanted to include a special section just for you to give you some of the principles and concepts that you will need to know to help you find (and be *sure* you have found) the right person to be your lifetime companion.

It has been said that our choice of a marriage companion can determine whether we will go to heaven or hell. After observing people and considering the subject for a long time, I am inclined to agree wholeheartedly. This decision must be made with much prayer and a great confidence in God's leading. For those of you who doubt that you can ever find the right person, I commend to you the following verse: "And we know that in all things God works for the good of those who love him, who have been called according to his purpose" (Romans 8:28). You must hold tightly to a few simple beliefs: God loves you; he is working out all of the details of your life according to his plan, and his plan is good.

Here are six principles—six tests for a serious relationship—that will help you as you seek God's will in this all-important decision.

The Test of Spirituality

> "But seek first his kingdom and his righteousness, and all these things will be given to you as well" (Matthew 6:33).
>
> Jesus replied: "'Love the Lord your God with all your heart and with all your soul and with all your mind.' This is the first and greatest commandment. And the second is like it: 'Love your neighbor as yourself.' All the Law and the Prophets hang on these two commandments" (Matthew 22:37-40).

These are the most important questions you can ask yourself about someone you are considering marrying:

- Does this person love God more than anything or anybody else in the world?
- Is this person seeking God's kingdom first in his or her life?
- Does being with this person cause me to love God more?
- Does being with this person cause me to love the church and other Christians more?
- Do we bring out the best in each other?
- Am I a better person with him or her than I am otherwise?

We know we have found the right person when our relationship enhances our relationship with God. To put it another way, being with this person draws us closer to God and more deeply into fellowship with God's people. In no way should our involvement with a person diminish our focus on God, his church or spiritual things. I love my wife with all of my heart, but my love for her flows in concert with my love for God and increases it. Never has my attraction or loyalty to her diminished my commitment to Jesus Christ.

Disciples of Jesus should date and marry only other disciples. Although there is no verse of Scripture that says that we could never be with a non-Christian of the opposite sex in a social setting, I can say that every power of logic would encourage us to go out with people to whom we can safely give our hearts. If you need conviction on the subject I would suggest reading passages like 1 Corinthians 7:39; 2 Corinthians 6:14; and Ezra 9:1-4. I want to spend my whole life with another human being who loves God supremely and will encourage me to do the same.

The Test of Compatibility

> Wives, submit to your husbands as to the Lord. For the husband is the head of the wife as Christ is the head of the church, his body, of which he is the Savior. Now as the church submits to Christ, so also wives should submit to their husbands in everything.
> Husbands, love your wives, just as Christ loved the church and gave himself up for her.... However, each one of you also must love his wife as he loves himself, and the wife must respect her husband (Ephesians 5:22-25,33).

The verses above describe for us the fundamental roles of husband and wife in the marriage relationship. As we begin to date someone, patterns emerge in the way we relate to each other. The biblical pattern is clear: The woman respects and follows the lead of the man, and the man loves and leads the woman. If the man does not have in his heart a deep love for and ability to lead the woman, the relationship is headed for trouble. Likewise, if the woman does not respect the man and cannot see herself listening to him, following him and being in submission to him for the rest of her life, then she should not marry him. This is not to say that some couples do not struggle in these areas, but it is to say that there must be a somewhat natural fit and that changes can be made rather easily.

Second, there needs to be a natural friendship between the two of you. If you marry, you will be spending the rest of your lives together; you certainly need to enjoy one another's company! There needs to be compatibility, comfortability and an ease of being together. It does not matter if you are very different in some of your likes and dislikes (many married couples wonder how they get along, considering their different tastes!), but your friendship and relationship should be a natural one.

Third, there must be a natural physical attraction. Sexual attraction cannot be the basis of your relationship, but it is important nonetheless. If a man and woman are not physically drawn to each other, how can they look forward to a lifetime of romantic love? You must find each other's basic physical appearance attractive. There may be some relationships where physical attraction is not immediate, but it must develop for the marriage to be fulfilling to both.

Having said this, let me say again that marriage cannot be based upon the sexual relationship or sexual desire. Oftentimes, people who are primarily drawn to each other by appearance are not able to put together a solid relationship because of other weaknesses, such as a lack of spirituality or an inability to develop an intimate friendship.

Last, I would say that both people must feel they are getting a good deal. I'm sorry, but I just don't know any better way to put it. For instance, if a woman thinks, "Wow, my fiancé is certainly getting a great deal. Look how attractive, good looking and smart I am compared to him," then please, don't do this poor wretch any favors by marrying him! Or if a man thinks, "I am a worthless, no good loser. This gorgeous, intelligent creature could be marrying someone a lot better than me." I beg you, get yourself together and start feeling better about yourself before you say "I do"!

The Test of Purity

It is God's will that you should be sanctified: that you should avoid sexual immorality; that each of you should learn to control his own body in a way that is holy and honorable, not in passionate lust like the heathen, who do not know God; and that in this matter no one should wrong his brother or take advantage of him. The Lord will punish men for all such sins, as we have already told you and warned you. For God did not call us to be impure, but to live a holy life. Therefore, he who rejects this instruction does not reject man but God, who gives you his Holy Spirit (1 Thessalonians 4:3-8).

Sexual purity must be maintained at all costs during dating and engagement. The sexual relationship is reserved for married people alone, and you are not married until the day you say "I do" in accordance with the laws of the land and in the eyes of God and his kingdom. The Bible teaches that the bodies of married people belong to each other (1 Corinthians 7:4). Your bodies belong to each other only when you are married and not before. Before you are married, your bodies belong solely to God (1 Corinthians 6:19-20).

If we allow sexual looseness into our courtship, we are destroying the very foundation of our future. We should refrain from touching each other in any area of the body that is sexually responsive or sexually oriented. Holding hands is one thing, touching our partner's body in an area of sexual stimulation is another. Included in this is the abuse of affection in ways like passionate kissing, French kissing and embracing that is overly protracted or too intimate. As we said in the previous section, there must be sexual attraction, but we must be careful to keep our attractions and passions in check.

To take sexual liberties before marriage is to show disrespect to each other. Believe me, after you are married, you will pay a price dearer than you can imagine for sexual sin beforehand.

Couples who do not have the maturity and conviction to maintain their purity with one another while dating have no business getting married. And if impure and sinful behavior is occurring in your dating relationship now, you need to immediately open up with other people about it and get help. If you are dating or engaged to someone who is pressuring you to go further that you know you should, you are responsible before God for your conduct, and you should take quick and decisive action.

There is nothing like the beauty of the wedding day of two people who have kept their relationship righteous. There is a sense of purity, joy and happiness that the world cannot understand! And there will be a far greater chance of a fulfilling and exciting sex life in the coming years in their marriage.

The Test of Longevity

Time is a great test for many things, especially for a dating relationship. It is easy for us to become infatuated when we first meet someone, but we will not know for sure if this person is the one for us unless we give it some time. There are several reasons for this.

First, you need some time to see people's weaknesses. You must see them not only at their best, but at their worst. Second, Before getting married to someone, you need to have had some disagreements and arguments and to have learned to solve them . Believe me, you will have plenty more after you are married! Third, you also need to have time to see how you relate to each other spiritually, and to see whether your influence on each other is a spiritually positive one or not. Fourth, if you are recovering from a recent breakup, divorce or the loss of a spouse through death, you need to give yourself some time. The desire for companionship may be so great that it blinds you. Some of us who are a bit older and more experienced might be able to make up our minds more quickly than a younger, inexperienced person, but even so, an appropriate amount of time must pass before we can be sure. It is better to wait a little longer and be sure than to rush things and realize later, with bitter regret, that we have made a mistake.

The Test of Society

Some couples get along famously when they are alone, but when other people come into the picture, they don't do so well. Sometimes we can meet someone, open our hearts to them, and they to us, and have some intense conversations that seem to indicate that we are one-souled and bonded for life. This may indeed be true, but we can be fooled. It is important to know how you relate to each other in the presence of others. Do you get along well in front of other people? If you find that you quarrel and offend each other, or that your partner does not want you to be around anyone but him or her, then I would suggest that something is wrong.

The other test of society is that we have dated enough people and have enough experience that we are confident we are making the right decision. If we live in a culture (as most of us do) where we have the freedom to make our own choice as to our marriage partner, we need to make the best use of this opportunity. I am afraid some of us have not really looked around that much and have jumped into the first relationship that offered itself to us. This is especially true of new disciples who are just experiencing the joys of God's kingdom. You have come in from the cold, cruel world, where you may have had many bad experiences with the opposite sex. Perhaps you, as a woman, were never treated kindly or in a gentlemanly fashion by any man. You are then swept off your feet by the first Christian brother who takes you out on a date, simply because he is polite. Or perhaps, you men have never felt respected by women in the world, and you are blown away by the courteous treatment you receive from the first sister you take out. You can automatically (and wrongly) assume this means that she is madly in love with you! You can conclude that he or she is the greatest thing that ever happened and that you must marry quickly before someone else beats you to the punch. What you must realize is that there are many other kind, decent brothers and sisters in God's church who will treat you the same way. Give them their chance as well! Don't fall in love after your first date as a new disciple in God's kingdom!

It is wise to have some acquaintance with your potential spouse's family before you decide to marry. How his or her family feels about your relationship should have no final bearing on your decision, but it is helpful in understanding their background. If there will be family resistance to your marriage or a severe cultural clash, you need to be prepared in advance. When you come from different backgrounds, you may have to make great adjustments to each other's past in order to forge a successful marriage. We know that the Bible teaches that we are all one in Christ, but family and background are important and must be taken into account. I would liken this to counting the cost before we make the decision to become disciples. We know that Jesus will be faithful to his word and that he promises a great life for us, but we must make sure that we are willing to put in the effort it will take and do our part in being his disciple. It is this kind of sober consideration that I urge upon you.

The Test of Economy

> In the name of the Lord Jesus Christ, we command
> you, brothers, to keep away from every brother who is
> idle and does not live according to the teaching you re-
> ceived from us. For you yourselves know how you ought
> to follow our example. We were not idle when we were
> with you, nor did we eat anyone's food without paying
> for it. On the contrary, we worked night and day, labor-
> ing and toiling so that we would not be a burden to any
> of you. We did this, not because we do not have the
> right to such help, but in order to make ourselves a model
> for you to follow. For even when we were with you, we
> gave you this rule: "If a man will not work, he shall not
> eat" (2 Thessalonians 3:6-10).

Marriage and love are an experience of great mystery and romance, but we also must be practical. We need to deal with the facts of economics. First, are both of you able, financially, to take on the commitment of marriage? If one or both of you are still in school, then you need to ask yourself if you can reasonably carry on your education while married. If your parents will continue to support you, that is well and good. If they choose not to do so, then you have a real decision to make. In my experience I have concluded it is wiser and bet-ter to get your undergraduate college education out of the way before marrying. I realize I cannot generalize too much on this subject, though, because it may be best for some to be married during school years.

This leads us to our second point: Is the man gainfully employed and able to support a wife? Women, let me say it plainly: A man should be holding down a job before you marry him. Never marry someone who has not proven himself to be a responsible worker who draws a consistent paycheck. Some women have lived to bitterly regret marrying a man who ended up being irresponsible, undisciplined and only wanted to sponge off his wife's hard work. It does not matter that a man is handsome, talented or can talk a good game. You want to be sure that he has a consistent record of work and wise fi-nancial management under his belt before you commit to spend the rest of your life with him.

Third, do both of you look at money matters in roughly the same fashion? If you come from widely different economic backgrounds, then the one accustomed to more money may need to prepare him- or herself for a life of greater frugality. If one person has the expectation of living the same high-income lifestyle he or she knew while being supported by Mom and Dad, it can lead to real frustration later on. Even though you love each other deeply, this issue should be considered in advance.

There is no way that I can adequately prepare you in a few words in a book to know how to make this great decision. That is where prayer and God's church come in. When it comes time to make this, the second most important decision of your life, you can use the help of God and his people more than ever. No one can make it for you—it must be your own, because you must live with it for good or for ill for the rest of your life. However, others can help you be more objective and to think rationally through this particularly exciting, emotional time.

I leave you with the story of Isaac and Rebekah as found in Genesis 24. Here the beautiful story of how God found a spiritual wife for the young man Isaac is recounted. Isaac and Rebekah were separated by hundreds of miles, and yet, somehow, God got them together. I believe God shows the same concern for every faithful child of his today as well. Abraham stated about God's guidance, "He will send his angel before you so that you can get a wife for my son from there" (Genesis 24:7). I believe that God will send his angels into our lives to guide us to the right man or woman. Our job is to prepare ourselves spiritually by being close to God, building strong character and developing a trusting heart. The God who created the universe and sustains it in its complexity and vastness, and who sent Jesus to earth to die for our sins, is quite able and willing to provide for us in marriage. May God bless you as you seek his will and the right person for your life!

Notes

CHAPTER 2

1. Alan Loy McGinnis, *The Friendship Factor* (Minneapolis: Augsburg Publishing House, 1979), 118.

2. McGinnis, 118.

CHAPTER 6

1. John White, *Eros Defiled* (Downers Grove, Ill.: Inter-Varsity Press, 1977), 37.

2. This is not to say that there are not marriages, or occasions within any marriage, when the wife may be more highly motivated and initiatory than the husband. What I have described are the usual problems and challenges and the basic dynamic of male and female arousal and response.

Life to the Full
A study of the writings of James, Peter, John and Jude
by Douglas Jacoby

True and Reasonable
Evidences for God in a skeptical world
by Douglas Jacoby

Raising Awesome Kids in Troubled Times
by Sam and Geri Laing

Let It Shine: A Devotional Book for Teens
edited by Thomas and Sheila Jones

Mind Change: The Overcomer's Handbook
by Thomas A. Jones

She Shall Be Called Woman
Volume I: Old Testament Women
edited by Sheila Jones and Linda Brumley

She Shall Be Called Woman
Volume II: New Testament Women
edited by Sheila Jones and Linda Brumley

The Disciple's Wedding
by Nancy Orr with Kay McKean

The Unveiling
Exploring the nature of God
by Curt Simmons

Mine Eyes Have Seen the Glory
The victory of the Lamb in the book of Revelation
by Gordon Ferguson

This Doesn't Feel Like Love
Trusting God when bad things happen
by Roger and Marcia Lamb

Quiet Time Books for Pre-Teens

"Follow Me"
First half of the Gospel of Mark
by Clegg & Betty Dyson

The Servant King
Second half of the Gospel of Mark
by Clegg & Betty Dyson

The Heart of a Champion for Kids
Spiritual inspiration from Olympic athletes
edited by Larry & Lea Wood

For information about ordering these
and many other resources from DPI, call
1-800-727-8273
or from outside the U.S.
617-938-7396
or write to
DPI, One Merrill Street, Woburn, MA 01801-4629
World Wide Web
http:\\www.dpibooks.com